WHEN Bourke Rold rode into
Canon City after his brother's killer—
he landed in the middle
of the railroad war
between the
Rio Grande and the Santa Fe.

Caught in the crossfire,
he went on the run—
branded as a deserter by the Army,
a killer by the Law.
But there was no place to run—
except into the killer's camp.

**Gun in hand, he moved in!
It was him—or the killer!**

CAST OF CHARACTERS

Bourke Rold meant to get his brother's killer —even if it took his own life.

Tom Kimbrell was dangerous and deadly with a crew of killers behind him.

Cass Ives, partner to two brothers—one dead, one about to be . . .

Ben Spohr had killed one man and Kimbrell wouldn't let him stop now.

Eleanor Hyde, spoiled, beautiful and desirable, she wanted Bourke—in one piece.

Kate Banks, her father had the clue to murder but she wanted the key to Bourke's heart.

ROYAL GORGE

by
PETER DAWSON

BANTAM BOOKS
NEW YORK

ROYAL GORGE

A BANTAM BOOK published by arrangement with
Dodd, Mead & Company, Inc.

PRINTING HISTORY

Dodd, Mead Edition Published September, 1948
1st Printing......................April, 1948

Lion Books Edition Published July, 1950
under the title *Guns on the Santa Fe*

Bantam Edition Published, March 1954
1st Printing..........February, 1954

Copyright, 1948, by Jonathan H. Glidden

All Rights Reserved

No part of this book may be reproduced in
any form without permission in writing
from the publisher.

The characters, places, incidents and situations in
this book are imaginary and have no relation to
any person, place or actual happening.

Bantam Books are published by Bantam Books, Inc. Its
trade mark, consisting of the words "BANTAM BOOKS"
and the portrayal of a bantam, is registered in the U. S.
Patent Office and in other countries. *Marca Registrada*

PRINTED IN THE UNITED STATES OF AMERICA
BANTAM BOOKS, 25 West 45th Street, New York 36, N. Y.

ROYAL GORGE

One

THIS WAS MIDDLE APRIL, well into spring of the year 1879. Yet all the grey afternoon the wind had howled in off the flats and now, at dusk, the Denver and Rio Grande's southbound local seemed to be finding its own way in on Pueblo Station across a smooth expanse of snow that hid main line and sidings.

When the pale eye of the *Huerfano's* headlight shone through the snow-fog, a Santa Fe guard left the station's cheerless waiting room and, carbine slacked in the bend of his arm, trudged out to stand in the lee of the telegrapher's bay. The wind muted the gathering hiss of steam and then the squeal of the brakes as the undersized four-car train slid to a stop abreast the platform. The guard stepped out into the gusts then, wanting to be seen and impassively eyeing the ragged lines of people straggling from the coach doors across the platform and into the station.

He saw one man—clad in a long buffalo coat and a full head taller than most of the others—step aside to ground a valise near the first coach's platform and idly look about. Because he was paid to anticipate trouble and deal with it, the guard at once sauntered over there and said dryly, "Move along."

Bourke Rold only half heard him and looked around in such a detached way that the Santa Fe man repeated, "Move along, friend."

With an effort Bourke brought his attention to the matter at hand, remembering. At every stop this afternoon the stations had been under heavy guard. Somewhat tardily now he realized the significance of this being Pueblo, chief strongpoint of a headline-making war between two railroads. Naturally no loitering near the right of way was allowed.

So he picked up the valise, drawled, "Sure thing," and started in across the platform. But he had taken only two

1

strides before his thoughts, shuttling back to their tedious channel, stopped him and he turned to ask, "How do I get across to Canon City tonight?"

"You don't. Last train's gone. Try the stage."

"How long does it take that way?"

"Friend, I'm new here. Ask inside."

Bourke said, "Much obliged," and went on. And the guard, eyeing his straight, broad back, thought, *Something on his mind.*

The waiting room was like a hundred others in the West, its scarred floor edged by plain benches, the potbellied stove giving out too little heat and ringed by men warming hands and backs, the boards damp around the unpolished brass spittoons and the air bad, stale with the taint of coal and tobacco smoke. Bourke Rold was only vaguely aware of all this as he stepped in behind a man at the ticket window.

He waited out his turn with an indrawn patience, his thoughts very far away, and when he moved up to the wicket the agent had to ask, "What'll it be?" before the vacant stare left his deep brown eyes.

"Anything going across to Canon City tonight?"

"Not till six-forty in the morning."

The agent was turning away when Bourke spoke again. "How about a stage?"

"No tellin'. One day they run, the next they don't."

"Where's the stage office?"

"Straight on out the street. You can't miss it." The man was at his desk now, head tilted and listening to the click of his telegraph key.

Bourke slowly wrestled with his problem, his mind too burdened with something else to give it full attention. Finally he asked, "Any horses for hire in town?"

"Nope. Only for sale. And for plenty."

Bourke unbuckled the heavy coat now and let it hang open, breathing a slow disappointed sigh. Quite suddenly he remembered something that livened the look in his dark eyes. "Have you anything for B. F. Rold?"

"Not a thing."

Bourke's look lost some of its warmth. "A telegram, I mean."

"That's what I thought you meant."

"Could you take a look?"

The agent all this while had been standing with his back to Bourke. Now he glanced around. "It's no use. I know what's come . . ." He paused, reached to his desk and thumbed through a sheaf of telegrams. "No luck. Now if your handle was Gold, you'd draw something."

"Gold?" Bourke echoed disappointedly. "Couldn't be B. F. Gold, could it?"

"B. F. it is."

Bourke's look became excited. "Signed Eleanor?"

"Sure enough." The agent came across and pushed the message under the wicket. "Give me a buck for every mistake like this and I'd draw double wages. This road's gone to hell." He was about to add to that when he noticed that this tall stranger was paying him not the slightest attention.

Bourke was reading:

MISSED YOU BY ONE HOUR AT HOTEL. PLEASE BOURKE PLEASE DO NOTHING UNTIL I SEE YOU. LETTER FROM FATHER EXPLAINS. YOU MUST GIVE UP THIS GAMBLE WITH OUR FUTURE. JOIN ME IN DENVER TOMORROW. WE HAVE PLANNED THIS FOR MONTHS AND I REFUSE TO BE LEFT AT ALTAR. TRIP FROM EAST VERY TIRING. I NEED YOU TERRIBLY. ALL MY LOVE DARLING. ELEANOR.

A slow smile softened the angular contours of Bourke's lean face. This wire, unlike Eleanor's letters of the past year, held an intimate quality that brought her very close to him. Its length was typical of her extravagance in everything. A momentary feeling of guilt erased his smile as he recalled how carefully he had planned missing her by exactly that hour she mentioned. Walking out on her had been one of the most difficult things he had ever done, so strong was his year-long hunger for the sight of her. Yet this other thing had outweighed his pleasurable anticipation then as it did now and, reaching to the end of the counter for a pad of blanks, he wrote:

MISS ELEANOR HYDE,
WINDSOR HOTEL, DENVER, COLORADO.

GO STRAIGHT ON TO POST. WILL MEET YOU THERE SOON AS POSSIBLE. NO CHANCE YOUR BEING LEFT AT ALTAR. MY BEST. BOURKE.

He read what he had written twice over, the banging of an express dray and the muffled, gradually fading blast of the locomotive's exhaust echoing in over the whine of the wind to distract him. The matter-of-factness of his answer annoyed him; but he had no flair for putting his feelings on paper and decided it would have to do.

He finally pushed the telegram through the wicket along with a silver dollar, asking, "Will that reach her tonight?"

"Maybe." The agent was staring out past Bourke across the waiting room now. As he made change he called, "Sidney!"

A youngster left the stove and came across to stand beside Bourke. The agent told him, "Something's coming through for General Palmer. Stick around and get ready to take it out to him."

Bourke had been only half listening. Yet the name the agent voiced had registered strongly on his consciousness and he asked, "General William Palmer?"

"The same. President of this line."

"He's here? Right now?"

"That's his private car down on the siding. Know him?"

"Once I did." Bourke was thinking, *Only that was long ago, fifteen years.*

He turned from the window and was halfway across the waiting room, his mind on Palmer, before he remembered the valise and went back for it. The room was almost deserted now. From outside came the squeal of the station van's iron tires and the muffled stomping of its teams slogging through the drifts toward the streethead. Bourke caught the sounds without their disturbing his inward absorption. He went out a door and was on the platform before realizing he had taken the wrong way to the street.

It was nearly dark now. The Santa Fe guard was still standing there and as his wary glance came around Bourke was feeling uneasy, knowing he shouldn't be here. He was reaching for the door again when he happened to look out along the twin furrows marking the line of the tracks. Off there a coach's lights glowed palely against the grey gloom. *He's right there,* he told himself, *less than a minute's walk away.*

The thought wakened near-forgotten memories in him —dimly he saw the images of troopers gathered about a feeble campfire deep in the dark hills of Tennessee, he glimpsed a dashing figure on a red horse leading a cavalry charge across a grassy valley; and, ever so remotely, he could hear the clear notes of a bugle sounding the Recall to end that charge. A loneliness as strong as his present loneliness was threaded through these memories. And now it struck him that he had been so wholly within himself that he remembered hardly one face or one spoken word over the past five days.

He was lonely, as lonely as he had ever been. And now, because he had no capacity for fighting such a feeling, the possibility of seeing a man even as slightly known to him as William Palmer became irresistible.

Obeying his strong impulse, he walked over to the guard. "I'm headed out there to General Palmer's car. Do I go alone or do you take me?"

"Reckon I'll have to take you."

So Bourke set his suitcase along the wall and they started on up the platform, leaving the lee of the station and walking head down as the wind took its bite at them. Bourke was feeling a new and strange light-heartedness at this pleasant prospect and now he spoke loudly, almost cheerfully over the rush of the wind:

"Don't they ever have a spring in this country?"

He caught the man's dry laugh. "If everything else's gone *loco*, don't the weather have a right to?"

Bourke understood. "So you're having your troubles. Who's paying you this week?"

"Santa Fe. Hired me away from the Rio Grande three days ago."

The high shape of a water tank loomed out of the darkness, its sides sheeted solidly with ice, and just short of it they swung over to a siding, the coach's lights a friendly strengthening glow against the blackness. Presently they could make out a group standing out of the wind close to the coach's rear platform, not a man in it who wasn't stamping his feet or swinging his arms against the cold.

At the foot of the steps the guard told Bourke, "Stay set a minute." He climbed to the platform and rapped loudly on the coach door.

His knock was answered almost at once. The door swung open on a burly, dark-garbed figure and Bourke heard the guard say, "Man out here wants to see the general, Mister De Remer."

Bourke recognized the name of the Denver and Rio Grande engineer as De Remer came out onto the platform and stared down at the indistinct shapes below him, brusquely querying, "Who is it?"

Bourke called, "Ask the general if he remembers a kid he let go from Anderson Troop at Prestonville back in sixty-four."

De Remer's face had worn a harried look Bourke was later to remember and understand. But now the man came close to smiling. "He'll always see a man from the Fifteenth Pennsylvania. Come on—"

His words broke off at the appearance in the doorway of a middling-tall and blond man clad in a long grey beaver-collared overcoat. De Remer at once turned to the newcomer. "You're satisfied this time, Kimbrell?"

The blond man laughed as he put on a wide hat. "More than satisfied," he said, and Bourke had the distinct impression that both the words and the laugh were trying De Remer's patience.

Then, when Kimbrell offered his hand and De Remer either failed to see it or purposely ignored it, Bourke was sure he was right about De Remer's mood. Kimbrell said, "I'll keep in touch with you." De Remer voiced a civil, "Do that," and then Kimbrell swung lithely down the steps.

De Remer stood watching until the man's bulky shape had melted into the darkness. Finally he looked down at Bourke, saying, "Come on in, Sir."

Bourke was only vaguely aware of the richness and quiet taste of the coach's interior as he followed De Remer in, for his attention was wholly centered on a straight, slight, full-moustached figure alongside a polished desk at the compartment's back wall. His recollection of Palmer had been hazy. Yet now it all came back. He was seeing that the years had aged the general but little. There was still the same alert look in the eyes, the same ramrod erectness Bourke had always coupled with his conviction that Palmer was the best cavalry officer on either side to come out of the War. And, once again, he was feeling that old intense pride at having served under the man.

De Remer said, "Sir, here's a man from your old outfit."

A warmth softened the questioning look William Palmer had focused on Bourke. He came out from the desk now, extending his hand. "I should no doubt remember you. But there were so many."

"The name's Rold, Sir. Bourke Rold. As far as I know you never heard it." They shook hands and Bourke added, "This gentleman was to ask if you remember the kid you kicked out of A Troop at Prestonville after that ride from Kingsport."

The general's puzzlement lasted but an instant, giving way to a quick smile. "Of course. You were under age, big even then. Had your sergeant fooled, unless my memory fails. Well," . . . He stepped back and took his measure of this tall, straight man . . . "that coat can't hide it. You've seen considerable of the service since."

"Since the next day, Sir, when they signed me on with Burbridge." This was doing Bourke good, this looking back. Some of the tightness was easing from his nerves and he was forgetting.

What he had said seemed to delight the general, whose smile broadened as he indicated one of the overstuffed chairs by the desk, saying, "Sit down, won't you?" Then, as Bourke was taking off his coat, De Remer put in, "I'll be going, Sir. Think we'll have much luck with Kimbrell this time?"

"Who knows?"

A look passed between the two and Bourke noticed that whatever De Remer gathered from it prompted him to a slow shake of the head. The engineer took his coat and hat from a settee by the door, said, "Good night, gentlemen," and was gone.

Palmer sat at the desk, his look grave now. He nodded that Bourke should take the other chair. "We're having our troubles," he said, "as you've doubtless heard."

Bourke only nodded and the other went on, "You would suppose that reasonable men could find a solution to the problem of two railways trying to build up that canyon to Leadville. Yet there's been nothing reasonable about it. Even the courts contradict themselves. Now we're both in the unenviable position of having to hire a gang of cut-throats to protect our rights."

Abruptly he straightened, the gravity going from his face. "But you've given me an excuse to think of more pleasant things. I see you're wearing a new suit of clothes. Which, by your looks, must mean that you're on leave."

"Not leave, Sir." Bourke tried to make his tone casual. "I've just resigned my commission."

Palmer was startled. "That's unfortunate. You were an officer? Cavalry?"

"Yes. Baxter Hyde's regiment."

"The finest in the service." The general waited and, when Bourke offered no further explanation, added, "You must have had good cause to leave it."

"I did, Sir. There was no trouble. No disciplinary trouble, that is."

"Could I help you in any way?"

Bourke shook his head. "Not that I know of, thanks. I was on the way through and happened to find you were here. Just wanted to pay my respects."

"I am honored." The general was obviously pleased. Yet something still puzzled him. "You're to be near here?"

"Canon City, far as I know now."

William Palmer was openly studying his visitor, trying to fathom what had been left unsaid, sure of his instinct for liking this man. Bourke's lean length had a look Palmer liked, the look of the born cavalryman. There was a hint of rawhide toughness in the broad, strong shoulders tapering to narrow hips and long powerful legs. The hands were long-fingered, strong, hands that could speak to a horse. But the dark brown eyes were warm and alive, almost merry, one moment and then deeply brooding the next. Worry, Palmer decided, more than ever curious over the unguarded and anxious look on that angular, tanned face.

This Bourke Rold had shown a stubborn streak in withholding the details of his resigning. But there was also an honest straightforwardness about him that now prompted the general to a final attempt at relaxing that stubbornness.

"Baxter Hyde is a reasonable man, Rold," he said. "I know him well."

"They don't come any better," Bourke agreed readily enough. "The fact is, with any luck I'll soon have him as a father-in-law."

"Really!" The general's smile returned. "I can remember Baxter's daughter as a child. She had spirit even then. My congratulations, Sir." A thought came to him that he knew he must express delicately in order to give no offense and he spent a deliberate moment in finding an approach to it. "Canon City is the center of our operations right now. We're badly in need of men over there, men we can trust. Could I persuade you to become one of them?"

"Railroading isn't my game."

"It wouldn't have to be. Am I right in assuming that your resignation will be hard on your purse?"

"Not too hard, Sir. A man can put something aside on a captain's pay."

"Still, with a wedding in prospect you might do worse than draw a salary while you're here."

Bourke thought that over quite carefully before drawling, "I'd rather not, Sir. This other will take all of my time."

What other? He hasn't said, the general mused. Aloud, he asked,. "Suppose this work for us wouldn't interfere in any way with your plans?"

He saw his guest start to say something, hesitate. To forestall a flat refusal he put in quickly, "It wouldn't take a minute for you to hear what it is." He rose from the desk and went to a door beyond the desk, opening it and calling, "Ed. Come here a moment." He looked across at

Bourke, half-apologizing, "That is, if you care to listen."

All Bourke could say without being impolite was, "I'd like to."

"Good." Palmer seemed strangely pleased that there had been no definite turn-down.

A man wearing a green eye-shade and leather cuffs at his wrists appeared in the doorway and Palmer, as Bourke rose, introduced him. "Captain Rold, this is Edward Jackson, one of our engineers. If you'll step on back to his office he'll tell you what I have in mind."

He indicated the door and Bourke, his coat over arm, went on through it and along a short hallway flanked by closed doors. The odor of cooking was strong here and beyond one of the doors he heard the clatter of a pan. At the end of the hallway he came to another office much smaller than Palmer's. It was shadowed, sparely furnished except for two straight chairs and a high slanting drawing-table over which hung a green-shaded lamp. A T-square, dividers, pen and a bottle of India ink sat on the board, which was covered by a survey map.

Bourke laid his coat on a chair, hearing the sound of Palmer's and Jackson's voices, low-pitched, coming along the corridor. He halfway understood that Palmer was trying to help him and the realization faintly angered him without in any way lessening his appreciation of the man's generosity. No one, nothing, was going to interfere with his reason for being here. Baxter Hyde had tried it, Eleanor was now trying. Much as he regretted having gone against them, he'd had no more choice with them than he had now with Palmer. He would, of course, turn down whatever offer Jackson was about to make him.

Jackson came on in now, closing the corridor door, saying, "Have a seat." As Bourke took one of the chairs along the wall, he sat on the high stool at the map-board, adding, "The general asked me to make his excuses. He's been called on in to town."

Bourke nodded, drawled, "Thanks. But this other is a waste of your time. I don't want it."

"So he said." Jackson's round face took on a smile. "It's a soft job, Captain. And the general would like to see you take it."

"Sorry." Bourke shook his head.

"Two hundred doesn't fall into every man's lap every month for maybe an hour's work a day."

No, it doesn't, Bourke silently agreed. It annoyed him to think that money could influence him one way or another, yet he was just now thinking of Eleanor, of how little he had to give her with his resignation on its way to Washington. Lately his thoughts had been too centered on the immediate future to have looked far beyond it. Yet he couldn't see a railroading job as influencing that future, so now he said, "That's neither here nor there."

Jackson took the stub of a cigar from the tray at his elbow and was careful to light it so that it burned evenly. "Well, I've got my orders to tell you what it is anyway." He gave Bourke a guilty look. "Providing you'll listen, of course."

"Go ahead. I'm in no hurry."

"We've had some bad luck up there near Canon with a tie contract," Jackson said matter-of-factly. "The Santa Fe got to one of our owners and bought him off, paid him a nice piece of change to buy up other subcontracts, then sell out to them." . . . He shrugged. . . . "We'd probably do the same with them if we had the chance. But now we've signed a new contract with this man. He delivers or we stop laying iron."

Bourke waited and shortly the man continued, "De Remer would like a reliable man, a complete stranger, to go across there and get one of Kimbrell's men to pass the word to him if the other crowd makes the same move again. You'd simply let us know and we'd take over from there."

"What else?"

Jackson shrugged. "That's all. You'd have to lay out a few dollars on whiskey maybe to get to one of Kimbrell's crew."

"Kimbrell?" Bourke was recognizing the name now. "The man that left as I came in?"

"Has he been here? They were expecting him. Good sized, light hair, moustache?" He caught Bourke's nod, went on, "He plays the gentleman and may be one for all I know. But last week one of our grade foremen called him for not delivering a load of ties. Mike wound up with a pair of busted ribs and some teeth missing. And Mike's as tough an Irishman as I know. So Kimbrell's able to take care of himself."

"That's all quite interesting," Bourke said. "But you'll have to find someone else to watch him."

"Suit yourself, I've done what I was told." Jackson took off his eye-shield now and, turning, reached down an overcoat from a hook on the wall. As he pulled it on he drawled ruefully, "Now I'll have to walk across there and tell 'em they can pull out with that work train. The general was holding it for you." He started for the door.

"A work train?" Bourke asked sharply.

Jackson nodded.

"Going to Canon City?"

"Where else?"

"Right now?"

"As soon as I tell 'em to pull out."

Bourke stood up, pulling on his coat. "Jackson," he said, "I'll take your job after all."

It was a five car train, three flatcars loaded with rails, one unheated coach and a caboose. As soon as Bourke was aboard, it pulled in off the siding and stopped at the station presently to load a gang of laborers. It took the bitterly cold coach perhaps two minutes to fill until even the aisles were jammed.

Just as the train jolted into motion, a burly, unshaven man in a sheepskin coat crowded through the door and began pushing his way along the packed aisle. Bourke, idly watching, took in the newcomer's barrel-chested build, his flat-crowned black hat and the belligerent way his glance was scanning the occupants of the seats.

Abruptly the man stopped alongside the second seat ahead of Bourke to say gruffly, "You there! Haul your freight."

The man nearest the aisle was undersized, a ranch hand by his looks, and Bourke heard him ask, "Why should I?"

"The seat's taken."

"Sure. I got it."

The newcomer's heavy-featured face took on a broad

expectant grin. "Now have you?" he drawled. He reached down and clamped a hold on the cowpoke's coat-front. Effortlessly it seemed, he lifted the man to his feet and swung him into the aisle. Then, ignoring him completely, he took the seat and sprawled low in it, tilting his hat down over his eyes.

The cowpoke grumbled something Bourke couldn't distinguish, there were a few laughs, and the crowd's attention wandered. But the man next to Bourke muttered to no one in particular, "Spohr will try that on the wrong man one day."

Bourke was no longer interested. He followed the belligerent Spohr's example, pulling down his wide hat to cut the glare of the overhead lamps and closing his eyes.

Several times as the train ran on through the night he dozed. But, awake, he couldn't help but overhear snatches of conversation. Now that he was working for the "Rio Grande"—as he constantly heard the railroad called—he paid some attention to what was being said, adding it to what he had read in the Denver papers this morning.

The D. & R. G., he gathered, had been leased to the Santa Fe to operate. Palmer was using the lease money to help build the new extension through a high-country canyon to tap the riches of the Leadville boom. The Santa Fe was building along the same route and each road was contesting the other's right to lay track with every weapon at hand—court fights, injunctions, armed crews, county politics. The Santa Fe seemed to be in possession of the Royal Gorge, its main work camps were located there. The Rio Grande had jumped to a point above what these men called "Twenty Mile" and were laying track fast along the upper canyon of the Arkansas. Bat Masterson, the Dodge City marshal, had recently been hired by the Santa Fe to bring in upward of sixty hardcases to cow the opposing forces. The Pueblo and Canon City stations were nothing but Santa Fe forts. Canon City, according to the talk, was a wide open town, a hangout for card sharps, promoters, women of questionable virtue and men of even more questionable.

Bourke hadn't seen Kimbrell board the train. But at the Canon City station as he was waiting to go down the platform steps he saw Kimbrell walk past in the crowd heading for the street. The man had probably ridden the caboose, Bourke thought, giving him credit for having chosen a warm spot for making the journey.

Somewhere between Pueblo and here they had run out of the storm. There was only ankle-deep snow on the wide street where cottonwoods coming into leaf edged the walk, lending an incongruous touch to the wintry scene. At this hour, just past nine, the town was still awake with a steady traffic moving between the saloons. The men Bourke met didn't look like townspeople. They were armed, walked singly and a good share of them had been drinking. Bourke sensed an air of tension, of suspended violence and wondered how long it would take for so many unstable tempers to light the fuse to real trouble.

For the second time in two days he signed a hotel register. The upstairs lobby of the *McClure House* was clean and freshly painted—as was his room back along the hallway—but he scarcely noticed the oddity of finding a good hotel in this isolated country. For his thinking had come alive once more along the pattern of the last few days, though now there was a slight difference. The waiting was over. He was excited and impatient as he asked himself, *How much more can he tell me?*

He laid his valise on the bed and opened it long enough to take out two letters and a heavy shell-belt and horn-handled .44. He spent a deliberate half-minute inspecting the Colt's, testing its smooth action and making sure that it was loaded except for the chamber beneath the hammer. He belted it on finally and, regardless of the prospect of going onto the street again, laid the buffalo coat aside. Then he picked up the letters.

One he kept in hand, thrusting the other into his suitcoat pocket. He left the room then and went back along the hallway to the lobby and across to the desk at the head of the stairs.

Glancing at the letter, he asked the clerk—an old man with tobacco-stained longhorn moustaches—"Where do I find River Street?"

"Block below toward the river."

Bourke nodded his thanks and started for the stairway.

"Any particular party you're lookin' for?" the oldster called after him; and without stopping Bourke answered, "No, much obliged." He had carefully thought out these details. It was important that no one should know anything about his errand.

He left the main street that was lined with brick-front stores and came to another paralleling it. Somewhere close ahead he could hear the muted, restless roar of the Arkansas flooding with snow-melt. He passed tree-shaded yards fronting prosperous looking frame and brick houses, walking fast to warm himself against the sharp bite of the still air. He was keyed up, almost in sight of the thing that had brought him all this way, and he thought with some surprise that he had missed a meal tonight; but he wasn't hungry. He was wondering about Eleanor again now, a small hope in him that she wouldn't go on as he had suggested but would wait for him in Denver. There in Pueblo before the train loaded he had gone into the station and asked that any telegrams for him be forwarded on here to Canon City. Whatever she decided, he knew he would hear from her.

Beyond the second cross-street he stopped a lone man he met along the walk, asking, "Where do I find Doctor Banks' place?"

"You're past it, way past. It's up the other way. Third corner you come to."

Bourke thanked him and walked back up the dark street to the third crossing. Here he had a choice to make. Only two of the four corner houses showed lights in the windows. The Banks place could be any one of the four.

So he chose the closest, opened the gate of the picket fence and started in across the yard, not noticing the shovelled side path until he was nearly to the porch. He walked across there and, when he was far enough to see past the corner of the house, looked back along the path to see a side door. Lamplight shining from the window of the adjacent house let him read a small sign over the door, Office.

He went back to the porch, a stronger excitement in him now. He was in luck so far. He knocked at the door and then carefully wiped the snow from his halfboots. The night was still enough for him to hear faintly a heavy tread moving across a room inside and he told himself, *He'll know more by now.*

The glass-panelled door swung open abruptly. It took him but a moment to recognize the square-built figure, nearly as tall as himself, standing outlined by pale lamplight shining from the end of a short hallway beyond. It was Kimbrell. The man was bigger, heavier than Bourke had realized.

"Yes?" Kimbrell said.

"Is the doctor in?"

"No, he's not."

"Any idea where I could find him?"

"Not exactly." . . . The hint of a smile touched Kimbrell's strong and ruggedly handsome features . . . "Doctor Banks passed away two days ago."

A shock ran through Bourke. Surprise and a bitter disappointment held him speechless. Kimbrell waited for several seconds, then said, "Sorry," and began closing the door.

"Wait!" Bourke could only think to reach out hastily and hold the door open. "How did he die?"

Kimbrell drew back half a step now. He was startled and increased his pressure on the door as he drawled, "The doctor made a hobby of rock climbing. He took a fall on one of his walks." He paused momentarily before adding with a deceptive mildness, "Now if you'll get out of the way, I'll shut this."

Some inner prompting cautioned Bourke against antagonizing Kimbrell. But his prospective relations with the man no longer counted. There were things he had to know just now, things far more important to him than any need for delicacy in dealing with Kimbrell.

"Did he have a family? Anyone I can talk to?"

"A daughter. But she's not seeing anyone tonight. The funeral was this afternoon. Call around again in a few days."

"Look," Bourke said with all the patience he could summon. "This is important. I'd like to see her now."

"You can't."

"Go ask her. Tell her it's something that can't wait."

Kimbrell shook his head. "Not a chance." He pushed the door shut a foot before Bourke could move to put a boot against it.

From beyond the hallway now a girl's voice called, "What is it, Tom?"

"Nothing." And Kimbrell added in a softer, more urgent tone, "Better be on your way, my friend."

But Bourke's mind was made up. Abruptly he edged into the opening, saying, "Let her decide. Just go ask her."

He was only slightly taller than Kimbrell and, looking across at him, he saw nothing in the man's expression to betray his sudden move. Kimbrell simply reached out and pinned him back against the door-frame with a solid hold. There was a lot of weight behind his big hand.

Bourke was already sidestepping the expected swing of Kimbrell's other fist when a shadow blocked the light from the hall and the same voice that had spoken before said sharply, "Tom! What are you doing?"

Kimbrell laid a hard grip on Bourke's arm, forcing him back into the doorway. "I'll handle this, Kate." His tone was deceptively mild.

Bourke half turned to see a tall, slim girl standing at the far end of the hall. He said, "Miss Banks, I've got to see you. Maybe it's the wrong time, but it can't wait."

"The hell it can't!" Kimbrell breathed.

"Let him in, Tom."

Kimbrell frowned and then slowly dropped his hand. Bourke took off his hat and crossed the hall to the room beyond where the girl stood waiting for him. It was a dining room. A low-hanging center lamp with a rose glass shade cast a warm light over golden-oak furniture. Knitting lay on the big center table. Beyond stood an ornate stove with a brass fender before it.

The girl was beside a rocking-chair close to the table now as Kimbrell, following Bourke, said, "I tried to keep him out, Kate. He wouldn't listen."

Kate Banks was watching Bourke. "It doesn't matter, Tom." She asked Bourke, "What is it you want?"

"Just a few minutes of your time, Miss Banks. Alone."

Kimbrell said softly, "No you don't!"

Bourke's glance was on the girl, noticing her paleness

and tiredness. Her words had been lifeless and there was a lacklustre look in her pale green eyes. She had good features and, Bourke judged, might have been passably pretty under more favorable circumstances. But now everything about her, everything but the sheen of her hair, was restrained and colorless. Even the hair, a rich deep chestnut, was drawn tightly back from her face and gathered in a Psyche knot at the nape of the neck. She wore a black dress unrelieved by any ornament, its high collar contrasting with her paleness, its plainness concealing the lines of her gently rounded upper body. Bourke remembered that her walk had been graceful. Yet now she lacked any strongly feminine quality that would impress a man and he was unimpressed as he said:

"My apologies for forcing my way in. But it's important that I see you."

For the first time now Kate Banks' eyes moved away from him to Kimbrell. "It's all right, Tom. You won't mind leaving, will you? It was good of you to come."

"I'll stay, thanks."

The girl gave Kimbrell the faintest of smiles. "Please, Tom. You heard him ask for Dad. I'll be all right."

Kimbrell stood as he was a moment. Then finally he came on past Bourke and took his hat and beaver-collared coat from the back of a chair along the far wall. He was ignoring Bourke completely as he said, "I'll be around in the morning, Kate. You may need something from town."

"You're very kind, Tom." And now the girl's smile showed a faint warmth in her as she added, "Good night."

She and Bourke stood in silence as Kimbrell went into the hall. Only when the door had softly closed did she turn and take the rocker, sighing audibly and then looking up at Bourke. "Now what is it?"

"I'm Captain Rold," Bourke began, not really thinking as he spoke and then deciding it wasn't worth the trouble to correct himself. He took the letters from his coat pocket, separating one from the other and handing it to her. "This letter of your father's reached me five days ago in Idaho."

She took a single sheet from the envelope and read it, at length looking up once more. "I don't understand."

He had been watching her closely and now as she spoke he had to fight back his disappointment. "The name Frank Ames means nothing to you?"

"Nothing."

"He was in business with a man named Ives. Cassius Ives. The Canyon Line, they called it."

She nodded. "Yes, I've seen wagons with that painted on their sides."

"That's it. It's a freighting outfit. Their yard is at a town called Spikebuck."

"Up the river. But you could hardly call it a town. It's only a small camp for the Rio Grande."

"You don't remember the accident?" he insisted. "According to your father, Frank drowned."

"Dad didn't talk much about his work. I helped him here at the office. But unless an outside case was unusual he would rarely mention one."

"Frank's case was unusual."

"Was it?" . . . The girl reached over to turn down the smoking wick of the lamp hanging low above the table . . . "The river's treacherous. Several men have drowned."

"But Frank was a good swimmer. And you're forgetting another thing your father says there. That it may not have been an accident."

Bourke held out the other envelope. "Frank never wrote, yet I had this from him two weeks ago. He was in some kind of trouble. His letter here says that if anything happened I was to know the trouble had caught up with him. Only that, nothing more."

Kate Banks put an elbow on the table and rested her head against her hand, no longer looking up at him. "I'm sorry, Captain. But I can't help you in any way. And I'm rather tired tonight."

Bourke knew he should be leaving. He was doing his best to rearrange his thinking to conform with this unexpected disappointment and the slow anger of frustration was building up in him. This girl must know something, even the hint of something that would help.

"Think, Miss Banks. It isn't reasonable you shouldn't know something about a matter your father considered this important."

"Perhaps not. But I don't know a thing."

"Can't you try and remember?"

Her head came up quickly and the green eyes showed anger and hurt. "Please, Captain. I've shown you the courtesy of listening when I'm unbearably tired and worn out. The least you can show me is the courtesy of not doubting my word."

"I beg your pardon," he said stiffly, the baffled anger in him holding on. "Did your father have some close friend who might know about this?"

She at once shook her head. "None I can think of. He was a very solitary man. Most busy men haven't the time to make close friends." She gave him an odd, speculative glance. "You're a very stubborn man, aren't you, Captain?"

He ignored her comment, querying, "Can you think of anything at all that might help me?"

"I've already told you I can't."

"You didn't ever hear of Frank? Not even by name?"

"Not even by name, Captain." The girl straightened and rose from the chair in a signal Bourke couldn't ignore.

He followed her to the door and spoke as she opened it. "I'll probably be at the McClure a few days. In case you think of anything. And you'd be doing me a favor if you kept this in confidence."

"I will. Do you want Dad's letter?"

"No. I can remember it." Bourke stepped out onto the porch and turned to her once more, saying perfunctorily, "It was good of you to put up with me."

She gave him a searching look and then asked, "Are you going to tell me who this Frank Ames was?"

He thought about it quite deliberately. Then he lifted his wide shoulders in a shrug. "Yes, if it makes any difference. He was my brother."

Kimbrell saw the door open, saw Bourke's high shape against the feeble light. He was standing outside the fence at the far corner of the yard and now unbuttoned his long coat, took it off and hung it from one of the fence pickets. Now the rise of anger at sight of the stranger warmed him against the sudden chill. He stood watching and once even shallowed his breathing, trying unsuccessfully to make out something Kate was saying. Then Bourke left the porch and came out the walk.

Kimbrell didn't move. He had picked his spot carefully, standing in the deep shadow of a locust thicket at the corner of the yard. He let Bourke get to within three or four strides of him before he stepped out to the snow-covered walk, saying, "Just a minute, stranger."

Bourke drew up short, making out Kimbrell's shape against the grey background of the snow. He looked the man over warily, his senses instantly tuned to trouble. He was particularly watching Kimbrell's hands. When he was sure they weren't going to move, he said, "My friend, I had to get in there and see her."

"No one pushes me around, ever. No one!"

If the man was carrying a gun, Bourke decided he didn't intend using it. No bulge showed along Kimbrell's thighs and the dark suitcoat was buttoned.

Some of Bourke's wariness left him then. "No one's trying to push you around." His tone was friendly.

"You tried!"

"Forget it." Bourke even smiled as he started on, stepping aside to go around the man.

He saw Kimbrell begin his lunge and tried to turn out of the way. But Kimbrell was too fast, striking out savagely and unexpectedly. At the last moment Bourke tilted his head far back and Kimbrell's fist only grazed the point of his jaw, solidly jarring his senses even so. He realized, again too late, how nicely this blow had set up the one that was to follow.

So he braced himself and took a hard right low on the chest. The wind soughed out of his lungs and for a full second he stood there paralyzed by the pain of his ribs, watching Kimbrell take a backward step and cock his shoulders for another swing.

Suddenly Kimbrell slipped against the snow. Bourke saw his chance and whipped his right hand up, then down. The heel of his hand caught Kimbrell, still off-balance, at the juncture of neck and shoulder.

There was no mercy in Bourke then. Kimbrell's gasp of pain marked the moment Bourke planted his boots wide and threw a second blow with all the weight of his heavy shoulders behind it. He hit Kimbrell full at the jaw hinge. The man's weight went suddenly loose. He fell slowly face down in the snow and his half-smothered breathing laid a muffled, sobbing sound against the stillness.

With a thrust of his boot Bourke rolled the stunned man onto his back. Then he leaned down and jerked the coat open, finding a short-barrelled .38 nestled in a holster at Kimbrell's left armpit. He threw the weapon far out across the street. Then he turned away and went on down the walk, not once looking back. And as suddenly as it had hit him, his anger drained away.

His thinking was a muddle now with everything gone wrong tonight. This meeting with Kimbrell made no more sense than his having come a thousand miles to talk to a dead man. This was the same brand of luck that had dogged him since the beginning, since Baxter Hyde's refusal to grant him leave on the grounds that what he proposed doing was foolhardy and dangerous. The only change in his luck had been that instant back there when Kimbrell lost his footing. Jackson had been right. Kimbrell was a fighter.

He asked himself what came next and found that he didn't know. He was exactly where he had been five days ago as far as any understanding of Frank's death was concerned. Doctor Banks might have known the answer he was looking for; but if he had, that answer had died with him.

He turned up to Main Street and, abreast the stores once more, idly noticed that the wide thoroughfare was now quite deserted. He passed a saloon, the *St. Julian*, listening to the tinny beat of a piano sounding from it. He was well beyond it before the thought of whiskey turned him about and took him back to it and through the batwing doors.

The saloon was small, crowded and noisy. He made his way to the bar and shortly was feeling a steady warmth settling through him. His chest still ached from that solid punch of Kimbrell's. Now he was regretting having made an enemy of the man and also wondering if he had hurt his chances of helping Palmer.

He stayed there at the *St. Julian's* bar a good quarter-hour, emptying a second glass that failed to lift him from his bleak mood. When he left the saloon his mind was idling, run down, and he was thinking only of how good a bed was going to feel after these long days and sleepless nights on stages and trains.

As he came even with a narrow passageway two buildings below the saloon, a voice spoke harshly out of the deep obscurity: "Hold on!"

He stopped. He wheeled to face the alleyway, seeing the vague shapes of two men already moving out at him. One held a levelled carbine. The other came out and around him and Bourke at once recognized the rough sheepskin coat. This was Spohr, the man who had helped himself to the seat on the train.

"It's on his hip," said the one with the carbine.

Spohr closed in on Bourke from behind, lifted his coat aside and jerked the .44 from holster. Then the other stepped in and pushed the carbine's barrel hard against Bourke's coat, saying flatly, "Just step back here, neighbor. And careful!"

Bourke looked down at the carbine. He saw the man's thumb curled over the hammer. The hammer was off cock.

He wanted a moment to think this out. "Back where?"

Spohr answered, "Where we can be by ourselves," and now moved up alongside, laying a hard grip on his arm. Bourke's gun was in his other hand downhanging at his side.

"Suppose I stay here?"

Spohr laughed. "Hear what he says, Bates?"

He was still speaking as Bourke's free arm slashed up, bringing the carbine with it. Bates' thumb couldn't move fast enough to beat the weapon's upswing. The next instant Bourke had wrenched it from his grasp and was ramming sideways into Spohr.

He drove Spohr solidly into the nearest wall-corner of the passageway, briefly pinning the man's gun arm. Before Spohr could free that arm Bourke's shoulder hunched hard into his chin. Spohr's head thudded with a skull-aching pound against the boards and in that instant of blinding pain before consciousness briefly left him his hands clawed open and he dropped the .44.

Bourke took a long chance now, ignoring Spohr's falling shape and wheeling in on Bates. A wild recklessness hit him when he saw Bates sweeping aside his coat. He hit Bates on the shoulder, rocking him backward. Then, as the man staggered into the head of the passageway, he threw out a boot and tripped him.

Bates wasn't quite down when Bourke dove on him, knees first. A sharp gasp of pain came from Bates as the wind was driven from him. Bourke's hand streaked under the man's coat, found a gun and whipped it out. He tried to hit Bates alongside the head, instead only raked his face with the barrel. Then the man was thrashing out from under him.

Bourke came erect and in the blackness could see nothing. He swung blindly with the gun again, missed, and took a smashing blow at the side of the head. He swung his free hand and his wrist struck numbingly across Bates' neck. He had his target now and swung another full blow to the face, struck again with the gun and this time connected solidly. He heard Bates go down the instant a slurring sound from behind brought him wheeling around.

There, lunging into the passageway, came Spohr. His hand fisted a Colt's.

Bourke at once sensed his advantage, hidden as he was in the blackness with Spohr silhouetted against the snowy street. He could have killed the man that moment but the thought never occurred to him. All he had to do was to step out of the way and let Spohr come even with him. Then he lunged, at the same time whipping the barrel of Bates' weapon down on Spohr's arm.

He heard the big man's gun spin against the boards of the building wall a split-second before his weight drove Spohr against it. He pushed away, dropped Bates' gun and tilted Spohr's head back with a sharp left uppercut. Then he hit with a full-driving right. Spohr fell into him and he stepped away, letting the man go down, knowing it was over.

He was winded, sobbing for breath and so suddenly played out that he had to spread his boots wide to stay erect. Yet there was something more he had to do, and shortly he reached down and took a hold on the front of

Spohr's sheepskin. Slowly he dragged the man's inert weight to the head of the passageway, stumbling, twice having to stop and rest before he stood in the open.

At the walk's inner edge he let go his hold on Spohr and leaned against the corner of the building, dragging in deep lungfuls of air and chuckling once as he saw Spohr stir and try to push up onto an elbow. He looked along the street to see that no one was in sight in either direction. Abruptly someone came out of the St. Julian and a brief, narrow wedge of lamplight shone out across the snow. The man went away upstreet.

Bourke saw his hat and gun lying there in the trampled snow close by and it was with a real effort that he trudged out and picked them up. When he lurched around again Spohr was standing.

Bourke strode up to him and Spohr cocked an arm and swung it feebly. The drive of his fist took him off-balance and he fell to his knees. Patiently, remembering what he had set out to do, Bourke took a hold on the man's collar and hauled him erect once more. Spohr made another weak attempt to hit him and then Bourke's patience drew thin. He turned the man and slapped him sharply across the face, twice.

"Listen!" he drawled. "We're through. I'm letting you go. D'you hear?"

Spohr mumbled something unintelligible. His arms were at his sides now, his face was bloody and his head sagged.

Bourke took a tight hold on his shock of dark hair and tilted his head sharply back. "Go tell Kimbrell it wasn't good enough. Get that? Tell him to send grown men next time."

Now, deliberately, he pushed Spohr around and lifted a boot to the man's backside. He pushed, pushed hard.

Spohr, nearly falling, somehow kept his feet under him all the way to the walk's edge. He teetered there a moment. Finally he stumbled and collapsed outward into the tierail beyond. The rail sagged, then split with a loud crack. Spohr went head-first into the slush at the street's margin.

Bourke carefully brushed the snow from his knees and turned away.

Two

A BREAKFAST FIRE burned its rosy hole through the shroud of before-dawn blackness at the Santa Fe's tent camp in the cottonwood grove along the river; and presently, when the sky was greying to the east, six men carrying rifles walked up through the snow and straggled onto the grade, climbing aboard a car of bridge timbers alongside the water tower. With the strengthening of the light their hushed monotones became larded with an occasional guffaw or bawled oath. A squat locomotive with a coffee-grinder stack coupled to the car started it up the grade and into town; the men sprawled out and made themselves comfortable. Passing the station they guyed their fellow workers guarding the barricades with profane catcalls and hoots of derision.

The train was making good speed as it breasted the grey walls of the State Prison beyond town. The men eyed the place silently, the morning's chill having subdued them somewhat. They were half frozen by the the time the locomotive slowed for the siding at Camp Judd some twenty minutes later in the Gorge; and when their car lurched to a stop they piled off and headed for a big blaze close by that was fed by discarded ties. The work crew and the freight wagons moved in on the flatcar and in another quarter-hour the wagons were loaded and their teams straining up the level grade dynamited from the cliffs along the river. It was full day now, the sun not yet in sight.

The town still slept. The first sounds after the locomotive's exhaust faded against the stillness were the cries of drivers hitching ox and horse teams to the big Conestoga freights strung out along the board fence of the corral between Fifth and Sixth on Main Street. The first of these wagons was moving off, headed for the Priest Canyon road to Leadville, when a calving crew of six riders, in off a trail to the north, turned out of Sixth past the Wet Mountain Valley Hay Store and rode down-street. Shortly they racked horses at the tie rail before the St. Julian, looking for a change from the frugal fare their cook had served them the past three weeks. One of Megrue's *Canon and Silver Cliff Stage Line* coaches slithered along the muddy street, the big Concord's two teams at a brisk trot as it made for the canyon road on the Fairplay run.

Bourke, standing at the window of his room, stretched lazily and yawned as he watched the stage go away. His years of waking with the dawn bugle had become too strong a habit to break. He was stiff and sore and the flexing of his muscles made him wince at the complaint of his ribs. His chin was tender, the skin there gashed so deeply he knew it would be hard to shave. But he had slept sound as a wintered-in grizzly and his mood was unaccountably lighter than it had been for days.

Now he thought back on the fight with Kimbrell last night, on his luck, remembering that free-for-all afterward and laughing aloud. The sound startled him. He hadn't heard himself laugh for too long.

It was a relief to find that the tangle of his thinking had somehow unknotted itself overnight. The fever of last night's violence had somehow burned out the core of his bitterness and just now he could tell himself, *Something'll turn up*, without the nag of worry, yet without forgetting Frank or his reason for being here.

He shaved, took a clean flannel shirt from the valise and, pulling it on, went back to the window and looked out over the town once more. The first strong sunlight was touching snow-blanketed roofs and the broad main street had come to life. Sometime during the night the back of the storm had been broken, there was a balminess in the pinon-scented air and Bourke guessed that the snow would be gone from this low country before the day was out.

The town, he saw, sprawled across a bay of these upper flats pocketing the mountains and presently he could make out a deep notch cutting westward through the cedar-dotted foothills, judging that it must be the mouth of Royal Gorge. Backing the lower tier of hills a line of stately white-hooded peaks thrust their shoulders into a high layer of cottony cloud, hinting at an awesome height. Bourke had heard a man on the train last night speak of those peaks as the Sangre de Cristos. Directly westward a broad wedge of blue sky showed below the cloud line to mark the pass through which the Arkansas roared down from the high country. It was the fight for that pass that was bringing all this early activity to the street.

Bourke was hungry, really hungry this morning and it was the thought of food that finally turned him from the window. He was buckling the gun-belt about his flat hips when sounds from the hallway turned him motionless, faintly startled. He listened to voices receding beyond his door, one a man's, the other a woman's. But then they became so muted that he finally shrugged away a thought that the feminine voice had sounded strangely familiar.

He was shortly pulling on his coat and picking up his hat when a heavy step came back along the hallway. As he was reaching out to open his door, someone knocked.

It was the old clerk he had questioned last night in the lobby, who now bluntly announced, "You got a visitor. She's waitin' for you in the sitting room there at the far end of the hall."

"She?" Bourke thought at once of Kate Banks.

"Some girl that just come in by stage. Good looker." The old man was turning away as he spoke.

The excitement Bourke had felt a moment ago at the prospect of seeing Kate Banks was instantly replaced by another, a headier one. He wheeled quickly out of the door and, broadly smiling, walked quickly down the hall. The end door on the right stood open. He paused at its threshold, the beat of his pulse quickening, seeing that after all he hadn't been mistaken back there in his room in thinking he knew that feminine voice. Sight of the girl sitting in the horsehair-upholstered chair at this room's window now did something to his throat—made it knot up and go dry. And when she turned, looking at him, he tossed his hat aside and went quickly toward her.

"Bourke!" she cried delightedly, rising from the chair.

Without a word he swept her to him, fiercely almost yet not hard enough; for she clung to him and when their

28

lips met her arm came around his neck, prolonging the kiss. Finally, when he drew his head away and looked down at her, she said, "Again, darling!" and he could feel the hunger in her stronger that second time.

He had to have his look at her and when he took her by the shoulders and pushed her away, glancing fondly down at her, she was smiling mischievously, gladly. In this moment, as always, Eleanor Hyde was quite beautiful. Sunlight blazing through the window laid an aura of gold about her tawny high-piled hair on which a ridiculously small blue hat was tilted sharply forward. She was dressed in the height of fashion, her dress of a deeper blue than the hat and exactly matching the color of her eyes. Her tight-cut bodice revealed a shapeliness of figure as near perfection as the delicate moulding of her face. She was small, somehow more fragile-looking than he remembered and that hint of womanliness he had last seen a year ago was stronger now, quite definite.

"I should know better than to be surprised." His smile was gone as he looked down at her. "But I am surprised, Eleanor."

"Foolish man. Did you think I could stay away?" She put her head to his shoulder, murmuring, "Oh, Bourke, I'd forgotten how good it feels to have you hold me. Why must you always hold back? Darling, we're to be married!"

"Who's holding back?" He laughed uneasily, her directness momentarily confusing him.

She looked up once more, serious now. "You're thinner, Bourke. And you look worried."

"No more than you'd expect."

She turned abruptly away and, taking him by the hand, led him to the big chair. She pulled him down onto its overstuffed arm as she sat in it, saying with a mock-petulance, "You're surprised, not glad I came?"

"Lord, yes! But I hadn't expected you. Thought you'd go on."

"You knew I wouldn't without you."

He chuckled in genuine amusement, remembering things about her that had escaped him over their year's separation. Her doing a thing like this was so typical he could wonder he hadn't thought of it, in fact planned on it. "Maybe I did," he said. Then, to cover that half-truth, he added, "You'll find your father in good spirits, Eleanor. He hasn't aged a day since you left the post."

"He never does." Her glance was studying him searchingly. "You have, though."

Bourke saw the way she was steering their words and shied from it. "Where's Gretchen?"

"In Denver. I saw no sense in bringing her down here when you're coming back with me today."

His deeply tanned face took on a definite reserve. Seeing that, she said, "You have to give this up, Bourke. It'll ruin you. You've never been like this before, so absolutely stubborn. Father said it came close to insubordination. Have you worked around mules so long that you've become like them?"

His slow smile told her nothing and shortly she went on, "So far you've done nothing we can't mend. Father's letter yesterday said he was holding your resignation. If you go back now everything will be forgotten."

"Can't do it, Eleanor." His voice was gentle but firm.

"But what can you hope to do here?"

"No tellin'. I've only just started."

"Started what?"

"Looking around."

"But for what, darling?"

"Frank was murdered, Eleanor." He spoke quietly.

She turned her head suddenly away with a hint of the vast impatience so typical of her mercurial nature. Then, as quickly, she was looking up at him again, a bright anger in her blue eyes. "Suppose someone did kill him! Wasn't he wild, always in trouble? And wasn't his trouble most always over a woman?" The way she said "woman" left no doubt as to her feelings toward Frank.

He had nothing to say and she went on in her forthright way. "Oh, I know it's not ladylike to mention such things. But they have to be said, Bourke. Frank was no good!"

"He was my brother, the only family I ever had." Bourke was wholly serious. "He raised me, Eleanor. Was father and mother to me. Why, most of the fun I can remember I had with Frank."

"He wasn't half the man you are."

Bourke drew in a deep sigh. "You're wrong. He was one of the best I ever knew, bar none. And he was straight, even if he was what you call wild. He would never have used a gun on a man's back. Yet someone just the same as used one on his."

"So you're trying to find out who did it?"

"That's about it."

She came up out of the chair with a nervous lift of her slight square shoulders. Had she been the same girl he had known a year ago he would have felt confident in judging her mood. But now he was unsure of reading it, for the year had worked as subtle a change in her manner as in her looks. She had matured greatly, and he sensed that her headstrong and unpredictable ways were no longer so pronounced. He halfway knew that she would somehow try to get at him now, to make him change his mind. But her way of doing it wouldn't be the old way.

He was therefore surprised when she swung from the window and came close to him. Her breast lightly touched his shoulder and she ran her fingers through his hair, softly saying, "Bourke, we can be married in Denver this afternoon. We can end this waiting if you'll only say the word."

"There's nothing I'd like better. But this other comes first."

"Then we can be married here. I'll wire Gretchen to come on."

He understood now that, having failed to make him change his mind, she would go to any length to saddle him with an obligation that would stop him from taking the risks he proposed. He gave her a glance that slowly lost its deep gravity and became gentle. "We'll wait, Eleanor. Until I finish this."

All the pretense left her now. But instead of anger showing in her eyes she looked down at him in an awed, almost frightened way. "What's changed you, Bourke? The only thing I've ever heard anyone say against you is that you're too easy going. Father said it in his fussy way. He was criticizing you as an officer."

Bourke shrugged. "There's no change in me."

"But there is." There was a wondering quality in her voice as her glance clung to him. Then in another moment she seemed to remember what she had set out to do and her look became almost calculating. She let her nearness, the physical contact, work at him as she sighed and looked around the room, murmuring, "I suppose I can put up with it a few days here. I'll get a room. Darling, I'm so tired. The stage jolted so that I couldn't sleep at all."

"Stage? They told me there wasn't one coming across last night."

That mischievous look he remembered so well touched her blue eyes now. "You're not a woman, Bourke. When the man at the station told me you'd come across to Canon City I paid a teamster fifty dollars to drive me across."

Bourke smiled meagerly, thinking how easily things always came to her.

"So I'll send for Gretchen," she went on, so lightheartedly that it was difficult to catch the mockery in her voice. "We can take rooms and she can look after my clothes. Are the beds filthy, Bourke?"

"Eleanor, you're not thinking straight. Denver's the place for you to wait. You could enjoy yourself. You'd be lost here with nothing to do. And I'll be on the go most of the time."

"Don't you want me near you, Bourke?" she humbly asked.

"Of course. But . . ."

Only now did he see the futility of arguing. There was more of her father to her than he had ever suspected and stubbornness was one of Baxter Hyde's better known qualities.

He stood up. "I'll see about rooms. You can have breakfast with me while they're carrying in your things."

She shook her head, smiling wanly, sweetly. "I'd rather just sit here if you won't mind too much, dear. I really am very tired. And I want to think about this. Ask that nice old man to come here, would you? I'll do whatever's necessary and then go right to bed. If you're to be around late this afternoon you might come see me."

This was her way of letting him know how much he was inconveniencing her. It was an appeal to his gentlemanliness, a last subtly barbed try at persuading him to her way of thinking. And it was a far different, more grown-up appeal than he had expected. Although her tactics were new and strange to him, such measures had brought her her way many times before and she was doubtless counting on them now.

But if she had changed, so had Bourke. He wasn't the man she had known at the post last spring. He had lost his carefreeness, he was in dead earnest where in the old days she had rarely glimpsed that facet of his nature.

That seriousness was almost frightening to her now as he stepped to the door without further apology or explanation. "I'll see if they'll let you have this and the adjoining room, Eleanor." His tone was polite but seemed to hold her at arm's length.

"Don't bother making the arrangements, please. I mustn't take your time. Just send the clerk to me."

He nodded, his look faintly amused, unreadable. Then he turned out into the corridor.

He stopped at the lobby desk, gave her message to the clerk and then, suddenly and guiltily deciding he didn't want to run the risk of seeing her at breakfast if she changed her mind, he went down and onto the street.

Going along the broad plank walk he was feeling uneasy over his parting with her. Always, until now, he had taken a certain pride in giving in to her slightest whim. It seemed fitting that a cavalry officer should be gallant, especially around the woman he had chosen. Summer before last at the post he had looked upon it as a privilege to cater to her wants, to her unstable nature he now could realize was a trifle spoiled even with its gloss of fine manners and niceties.

If Eleanor Hyde had once been desirable, she was more than ever so now. Her new-found womanliness became her well and now he saw her as being utterly feminine, as having outgrown a certain tomboyish quality that life on various posts had given her. Mrs. Fullbright's Academy for Young Ladies had been a good investment for the colonel. His daughter had become a lady.

Over this past year Bourke's every hope and plan had been woven about this girl. It filled him with a pleasurable excitement now to realize she was even more desirable than he had imagined her. Their meeting this morning was something he would always remember, their later disagreement something that could easily be smoothed over. And with any luck they could start back to the post in a few days. No, it wouldn't be wise for them to marry in Denver. Baxter Hyde was a stickler for the formalities.

Bourke immediately felt better as these thoughts came to him. His mind was relieved and, gradually, he became aware of his surroundings. Close ahead he spotted the sign of a restaurant. He was stepping around a barrel filled with new-painted hoes and rakes and shovels standing in front of a hardware store next to the restaurant when he saw Spohr.

The man was leaning against a post of the walk-awning fronting the building beyond. He had shaved this morning, yet the dark pattern of his beard plainly shadowed his swarthy face. His lips looked puffy and along one cheekbone ran the livid line of a deep cut. He was idly watching the people on the walk, his sheepskin coat hanging open, thumbs hooked in a shell-belt that sagged from his thick waist.

Bourke had paused before the restaurant door, and was reaching for it when he saw Spohr's glance swing this way and come sharply alive. He let his hand fall and turned slightly, facing the man. Spohr's eyes veiled over as he took in the move and understood it. He looked away then and indolently pushed out from the post and strode on down the plank walk. When he had gone on a dozen strides, Bourke went into the restaurant.

Kimbrell wakened a little later than Bourke and, like Bourke, the first thing he did was to go to the window of his top-floor room in the hotel and look out across the town. But his inspection was no idle one as Bourke's had been.

Far up River Street he made out the leafless tracery of

locust trees and, through it, the roof of the Banks house. There was smoke coming from one of the chimneys. This seemed to satisfy him, for he left the window and dressed hurriedly. Then, even though he was hungry, he walked on down the cross-street and up to the second corner of River and around to the kitchen porch of the doctor's house.

Kate opened the door as he was stomping the wet snow from his wedge-heeled boots. She was obviously surprised at seeing who it was. "Tom, the roosters are hardly through crowing! You're so early!"

His blocky face took on a sheepish smile. "My conscience, Kate. It wouldn't even let me eat breakfast."

Her look was puzzled. "What have you done?"

"Made a fool of myself."

"How?"

"Last night. Buttin' into something that wasn't my affair. I came to apologize, Kate."

"Because you tried to keep Captain Rold from seeing me?" Kate burst out laughing at his contrite expression. "You did as you thought best."

"Then I'm forgiven?"

"Of course. So now you can enjoy that breakfast." She hesitated, looking back into the kitchen. "If you're not too particular, there's a crock of buckwheat batter and the griddle's ready as soon as the coffee boils."

Kimbrell smiled in that infectious way he had, drawling, "No, I'm not too particular." And when she turned in the door he followed.

Kate looked more like herself this morning, Kimbrell noticed. Her hair was done the way he liked it, loosely so that it showed its gentle curl and braided with the deep copper coils circling her head high in front and low at the back. She was wearing a pale green gingham house dress, a yellow and white-checked apron over it. She had color in her cheeks and her leaf-green eyes were alive, sometimes merry, not showing their deep hurt of yesterday. She and her father had been very close. But she wasn't letting her loss tear her apart as it had threatened to last night.

Watching her move to and from the table Kimbrell was suddenly struck by a thought that hadn't until this moment occurred to him. Kate Banks was uncommonly attractive. This notion was altogether disconcerting, so foreign was it to his reason for having cultivated her acquaintance.

Until these past two weeks he had known the girl only slightly; and in getting to know her better he had been so wholly engrossed in a strictly private motive that he had been hardly aware of her as a person. That motive was what backed his reason for being here this morning, and it quite possibly concerned this stranger, Captain Rold. He would learn what he had come to find out in due course. Meantime, he was realizing he had overlooked something.

He deliberately thought out the best way of leading up to what he had to say and finally had it. "Kate, what happens now? Will you stay on here?"

She came across from the stove and filled his cup from the steaming pot of coffee, her expression serious. "Haven't decided yet, Tom."

"Didn't the doctor have a brother?"

"Yes. Back in Kansas. They'll want me to be with them. But for a while Dad's patients will keep coming. I can't just up and leave until another doctor comes in."

"But you're alone in this big house, Kate."

She laughed. "And very able to look after myself. The Whipples next door are keeping an eye on me."

He watched her go back to the stove and ladle thick buckwheat batter onto the griddle. He was noticing how well-poised she was, the sure way her hands moved. And his interest stirred more fully as he took in the strongly feminine moulding of her tall figure. He decided to come out with it.

"Any prospects of marrying, Kate?"

She looked quickly around at him, broadly smiling and her color deepening. "No, come to think of it. About the only men I've seen have had something wrong with them. Cuts or broken arms and the like. They're generally feeling too sick to notice me."

"My arm isn't broken, Kate. And I'm not a sick man."

She eyed him steadily a moment, her smile holding but its quality subtly changing to a mischievousness. "No. But your face is swollen and red there by your right ear, Tom."

His pale grey eyes came brightly alive. It took him a

long moment to hide the anger. He laughed uneasily. "Maybe I better own up to it. I waited out front last night. Had a few words with your friend. He . . . well, he got in a lucky punch."

"You fought?" She was incredulous. "Why?"

Kimbrell picked up his cup and took a careful sip of the hot coffee. "Guess I'm just knot-headed, Kate. He pushed his way in."

"But he had a reason, Tom. You should have let him in when you saw he wouldn't leave."

Kimbrell lifted his heavy shoulders. "It would take a really good reason to bust in the way he did."

He waited for her to answer that. But Kate only turned back to the stove, saying nothing. They had been talking around the edges of the thing he had come here to get an answer to. When he spoke again he tried to make his tone casual. "What was it? I told him about your father. So he couldn't have needed doctoring."

"No."

That was all Kate had to tell him. And as he sat there trying to see a way of tactfully making her explain further, she came across from the stove with a plate stacked with buckwheats, telling him, "Dad always liked them three at a time. And he always took at least two helpings. You won't be invited again unless you do the same, Tom."

There was no further opportunity for Kimbrell to bring up the subject of the stranger and, half an hour later when he left, he was in a restless and angry mood salted with a touch of real concern. Kate had not only succeeded in turning flat his near proposal of marriage but had kept from him the answer to something he needed to know. Why had she been so secretive about the reason for the stranger's call last night? She had called him Captain. Now he was remembering Bourke's erect bearing, the way he held his shoulders, and was asking himself, *What business would the old sawbones have with an Army man?*

Spohr, impatiently idling at the doorway to the office-shack at Kimbrell's lumber-yard, saw him coming and walked on up the street to meet him. As he approached Kimbrell he caught the angry set of his face and wondered if it could be the memory of last night that was still rankling.

"Your man's down there at Uncle Tom Pennington's place havin' breakfast."

Kimbrell stopped short. "Alone?"

Spohr nodded. "And not afraid, either. Squared away at me like he was ready any time I was. Want me to get back there and keep an eye on him?"

"No." Kimbrell had been too preoccupied to remember his after-breakfast cigar. He thought of it now, took one from his pocket and, as he bit the end from it, decided something. "I'll have a talk with him."

"What the hell for?"

"I'm not at all sure what for, Ben." And Kimbrell wasn't.

They walked together as far as the shack where Kimbrell said, "Stick around till I get back," and went on.

He found Bourke at one of the restaurant's small rear tables. As he walked straight back there, Bourke lazily came out of his chair and moved it away from behind him.

"Sit down, Captain. I came to have a talk with you." Kimbrell pulled out the chair across the table and sat in it. His manner was disarming, almost friendly.

Bourke stood looking down at him. "You could have talked last night."

Kimbrell grinned guiltily. "So I could. Guess I was carryin' a big head of steam. Like you tried to tell me, 'Forget it.'"

Bourke moved his chair against the wall and eased his lean length into it obliquely facing Kimbrell, saying nothing, waiting. He pushed his empty plate away and took out his pipe, packing it with tobacco from a buckskin pouch.

"You know how it is when a man's courting a girl," Kimbrell said to break the awkward silence. "Sometimes he can't think straight."

Bourke nodded, still waiting.

Kimbrell was thinking, *He's got a damned cool head on him*, as he drew on his cigar. "I'm trying to help Kate with her affairs. Maybe if I'd told you, you wouldn't have asked me to leave."

"Maybe not."

"What was it you came to see her about?"

"Ask her."

"I did."

Bourke realized then that by making an issue of this thing he was only whetting Kimbrell's curiosity. And the one thing he didn't want was for Kimbrell, or anyone else, to become curious about him.

"So she wouldn't tell you?" He waited for Kimbrell's shake of the head, then chuckled. "She wouldn't. She's too proud."

"What about?"

"Money."

Bourke saw some of the wariness instantly leave Kimbrell's pale grey eyes. And when Kimbrell spoke the edge was gone from his voice. "So that's it." He was watching Bourke closely now. "How come you couldn't wait till today to see her?"

"And be the last in line?" Bourke shook his head. "The old man didn't leave much. I was after mine before the rest got theirs."

Kimbrell's relief was so keen that he gave a gusty laugh, seeing the irony of all his worry. So, after all, nothing but cold-blooded gall lay behind the stranger's visit last night!

I could use his brand of guts was the thought that struck him then. Here was a type of man who appealed to him. Ben Spohr had some of that same gall, a cruder kind. And maybe there was some of it in Kimbrell's own make-up. But he doubted that he would have had the calculation or nerve to do what this stranger had done, force his way in on a girl the night of her father's funeral, not letting her feelings stand in his way.

"So now you've got your money," he mused. "What do you do with it?"

Bourke saw that his lie had carried nicely, that Kimbrell was in fact showing him a grudging admiration. So he decided to play out this part he had stumbled onto. "Hang onto it," he drawled. "Make it work for me."

"She called you 'Captain.'"

Bourke nodded. "On leave of absence. Army."

"For how long?"

Bourke shrugged. "Haven't read my orders yet."

Kimbrell had known one or two deserters in his time and now reasoned, *He may open up to me some time. Then I'll have him.* Aloud, he asked, "Want a job?"

"That depends."

"On how good it is? This one would be good."

"How good?"

Kimbrell was watching Bourke touch a match to his pipe as he answered, "If you could put up a thousand, say, it might get you two. Or even three."

"Might."

"All right, come look it over. Decide for yourself."

"What do I look over?"

"Lumber. Ties and bridge timbers."

Bourke eyed him levelly for several seconds, finally took the pipe from his mouth and drawled, "Did I say I had the rest of my life to make a stake?"

"Did I say it would take you that long?" Kimbrell carefully countered.

Bourke's look was enigmatic. "Maybe I'll be around. Where do I find you?"

"My yard's up at the north end of town. Anyone can tell you." Kimbrell hesitated, then asked, "What's wrong with coming along now?"

"I've got a couple of other things on the fire."

Kimbrell, catching a faintly amused glint in Bourke's eye, had the hunch just then that this big easy-going man was somehow baiting him. That rankled, and with a sudden impatience he said the first thing that came to mind. "You were damned lucky last night, Rold."

A spare smile broke through Bourke's impassiveness. "I usually am."

"So am I. Get that straight." There was a strong belligerence showing in Kimbrell. "By the way, I'm out a new thirty-eight I was wearing when I ran into you."

"You can dig around for it in the snow across the way from where we were."

Kimbrell didn't like the sureness of this stranger's tone, nor the way a hint of the smile stayed in his eyes. But now he caught himself, knowing he was a fool to be spoiling any chances he might have with Rold. His glance lost some of its truculence as he rose and looked down at Bourke, saying, "Think over the offer. Between us we might travel quite a piece."

"Don't count on it, friend," was Bourke's reply, and Kimbrell turned away.

Watching the man's broad back as he went out, Bourke's feelings were not nearly so placid as the set of his features indicated. Without much effort—simply by wording a lie that was hurting no one—he had satisfied Kimbrell's curiosity and perhaps laid the groundwork for doing a job for Palmer and the D. & R. G. If he could string Kimbrell along by being friendly it should be a fairly simple matter to uncover the information Jackson wanted and pass it on. Meantime he would stay away from any involvement with Kimbrell and go on with the thing that had brought him here, trying to uncover some trace of Frank's killer.

Presently he paid for his meal and loafed out onto the street to stand at a spot along the walk's edge where the snow-melt had left the planks dry. The strong sunlight was taking the early chill from the air and he felt good, restless to be doing something. The next thing, he supposed, was to find Cassius Ives, Frank's partner. He stood there for several minutes trying to think of a way he could approach the man and something he had said to Kimbrell, ". . . a couple of other things on the fire," finally gave him the start of an idea.

Why couldn't he call on Ives as a prospective buyer of the half interest in the business that had been Frank's? He would, of course, keep his identity strictly to himself. Since Frank had been living here under an alias, it was a fair bet that the name Rold would mean nothing to Ives.

Ever since the day after they had pulled Frank's body from the river—the day after the inquest—Cass Ives had conscientiously and methodically gone about the task of determining the state of his and his late partner's material affairs. Some days—like yesterday with Dan Exin gone and a multitude of detail in the yard needing his attention—he would make only an entry or two in the black ledger he had titled, *Canyon Line, Its Holdings, Inventory and*

Liabilities. Today he had expected would turn out much the same as yesterday, over-crowded.

But now with the noon meal an hour gone there came an unlooked-for letup in his routine. His desk was average clear of work, he could hear the ring of Jim Manlove's anvil as the blacksmith shaped new tongue-irons for the wagon they'd pulled from Cottonwood Gulch and were rebuilding, young Ira Gaines was cleaning the end stables vacated by the Lookout Mountain teams and Charley Wong, the cook, would be taking his siesta on the counter in his kitchen. Dan Exin, the foreman, was due back any minute now with that wagonload of supplies he'd driven to Canon to get yesterday. But until Dan pulled in there was nothing to do.

So Cass tucked the ledger under his arm, took pen and ink and left the office to pick the bare-branch shade of the yard's one tree, a Russian olive, as the best spot from which to survey the lot and do his work. He judged it would take him no longer than an hour to make an over-all inventory of the yard's buildings.

He was a small man standing barely five-foot-three in wedge-heeled boots. A bushy black beard cut spade fashion and showing premature streaks of grey made him look both older and more belligerent than he was, for he hadn't yet reached thirty-eight and was ordinarily mild-mannered. It was typical of his orderly thinking that he had set about his task. One day soon lawyer Dean in Canon would be out here wanting to discuss things on behalf of Frank's family and Cass intended he should know what he was talking about when that happened.

The entries already logged in the ledger had mostly been annoyingly detailed items such as, "14 Peter Schutler Wagons, hickory, each with two spare wheels, one spare axle, hardware, etcetera . . . value——," or "Haying equipment, location Wet Mountain Valley Lease, West Homestead . . . value——," or even "Veterinary Tools, Supplies, Medicines, etcetera . . . value——." Now it was pleasant to begin at the back up-river corner of the yard and make a bold entry such as, "Barn, roofed, not walled, two-storey, measuring approx. ninety by thirty feet . . . value——."

Cass made an entry for each building in its proper order running the line of the west fence. To this side of the barn lay the square pole corral; then came the eight double-doored stalls, the open-fronted wagon sheds. Along the front—flanking the road that ended two hundred yards below at the tent camp where lived the Rio Grande guards manning De Remer's stone forts that kept the Santa Fe at bay in the Gorge—were only the slab fence, gate, office and a stack of split pine and cedar Cass estimated would run to eight cords. Down the east fence line he made entries for bunkhouse, mess shack and kitchen lean-to, storage shed, blacksmith shop and water tank. Then he happened to remember the baled hay in the barn's loft. He was eyeing the filled loft, trying to estimate the tonnage, when he saw the rider coming down the steep twisting trail out of Spikebuck Canyon beyond the barn.

He supposed at first that Bourke was headed for De Remer's camp. Men came and went from those guard tents at all hours of day and night, since it was both a shortcut from the Leadville road to the Santa Fe grade in the Gorge and a natural stopover for any Rio Grande man riding horseback to Texas Creek and beyond. So he went on with his work, idly listening to the hoof-clatter of Bourke's horse. Only when he heard the animal turn in at the gate did he glance around.

Bourke saw him sitting there and came on across until he reached the tree's dappled shade before swinging aground. As he dropped the reins, Bourke drawled pleasantly, "Afternoon. You wouldn't be Cassius Ives?"

"I am."

Ives stayed as he was, sitting, giving way to a life-long habit of never letting his smallness of stature contrast strongly with a tall man's unless absolutely necessary.

Bourke gave his name, which meant nothing to Cass. Then he said, "Came out on the off chance you're looking for a new partner, Ives. They told me about Ames in town. That was bad luck, your losing him."

"Worse than you'll ever know," Cass said.

He glanced up at Bourke in a measuring way, for the moment instinctively liking his looks. Then, oddly, the thought struck him, *He must be a Kimbrell man*, and he was at once annoyed and half angry. Tom Kimbrell had over the past months made several offers of buying Canyon Line. He was, in fact, the only man who had ever tried to buy the outfit. Frank had never liked him, had been dead set against selling to him. And now Cass, who had at first felt neither one way nor the other about Kimbrell, had come around to Frank's way of thinking, objecting strongly to Kimbrell's ready assumption that anything he fancied was his for a price.

So, sure of his hunch about this stranger, Cass now went on, "I'm afraid you've had yourself a ride for nothing. The layout's not for sale."

"Not even Ames' interest?"

"No. First place, his kin may not want to sell. They haven't been heard from yet. And if Frank's half is offered I may buy it myself."

Bourke grinned disappointedly. "Just my luck to hear of a good thing and run onto a snag right away."

It was only to be making conversation that Cass said, "You could buy into any number of things in Canon."

"Not horses, though. I'm fresh out of the Army. Horses are the only thing I know."

Cass shrugged, said nothing; and shortly Bourke went on, "Just suppose I might have a chance at Ames' half the business. What price would you put on it?"

Cass gave a slow shake of the head and reached over to slap the ledger sitting across his knees. "A week from now I might be able to answer that. This is the first chance I've ever had to get a line on exactly what we have. Up till now we've been too busy to take stock. We've bought what was needed and to hell with our inventory so long as we made money."

"About what I expected," Bourke drawled. All at once his look brightened. "Then how about this, Ives? Give me a sixty day option on Frank Ames' share of the business providing it's put up for sale to any outsider. I'd be willing to pay a hundred for such an option."

Cass was listening, though his glance had gone out beyond the barn and up the deep slot of Spikebuck. A moment ago he had heard the far off mutter of hooves echoing out of the canyon and, eyeing the trail now, he saw two riders headed this way along it. And suddenly the strong urgency of alarm ran through him as he recognized the pair.

Tom Kimbrell's wide shape was as unmistakable to him as Ben Spohr's.

Over the next few seconds Cass did his best to hide his panic. Already convinced that Bourke was a Kimbrell man, he now became even more convinced that some sort of trouble was in the making. Kimbrell wanted the yard badly; freighting his own ties he would have practically a monopoly of the business and could ask almost any price of either railroad. With no luck so far in getting his hands on Canyon Line in the accepted way, the man might today be resorting to the strong-arm tactics it was rumored he had used in forcing his tie-camp competitors to sell out to him.

What would happen during the next several minutes, Cass had no way of knowing. But he definitely saw a trap here. He wished almost prayerfully that Dan Exin would drive down the road. The yard was practically deserted, this stranger was already on hand to keep him from summoning help and now Kimbrell and Spohr were on the way in to finish whatever deviltry Kimbrell had thought up.

Cass did some quick thinking then. One more look at Bourke, at the .44 sagging along his flat thigh, told him that this stranger was very possibly more dangerous than either Kimbrell or Spohr. He himself was unarmed, his Colt's lying as usual in the top drawer of the office desk.

So now, thinking of the weapon and remembering Bourke's offer, he said, "That's a fair proposition. I can use the hundred. Come on in and we'll write up the option." And he came erect, leading the way over to the office.

He was well ahead of Bourke on entering the shack and went straight through the gate in the railing and was standing behind his desk, the drawer open and the Colt's lying within easy reach, by the time Bourke came in the door. Then for a moment he was uncertain, wondering what came next. In the end he decided to play the thing through the way they were calling it. He took his chair, picked up a pen and began writing.

He was still writing when Tom Kimbrell and Ben Spohr came in the door a good two minutes later.

Kimbrell had the time to say cordially, "Hello, Ives. Where's the rest of your—" before he noticed Bourke and abruptly stopped speaking. Cass noticed that hesitation, understanding it no better than he understood the dryness in Kimbrell's tone as he shortly drawled, "You again," looking at Bourke.

Ben Spohr's reaction gave Cass even more definite evidence that he had been mistaken in thinking the stranger a Kimbrell man. For now, at sight of Bourke, Spohr stepped in behind Kimbrell and furtively swept his sheepskin coat clear of his right side in a gesture that telegraphed an unmistakable meaning.

For the next several seconds as the room's stillness hung on, a vast relief settled through Cass. He was no longer afraid and, to convince himself even more thoroughly of how mistaken his hunch had been, he pointedly asked, "You gents acquainted with each other?"

"We are," Bourke drawled, a faint smile on his lean face.

Kimbrell now sensed the move Spohr had made and half turned to his man, snapping, "Come off cock, Ben." Then he made a visible effort to appear more at his ease. His glance came around to Ives and he was pointedly ignoring Bourke when he asked, "Got a minute to talk something over, Cass?"

"Sure. Go ahead."

Kimbrell's hesitation made it obvious that he wasn't much liking the stranger being in on this. But after a moment he must have decided to make the best of an awkward situation, for he said, "That deal I made for the Cottonwood haul has bogged down, Cass. This man's equipment is too light and too old for the job. I want you to take it back."

Cass at once shook his head. "Can't do it. And you know why. We're through with night hauls. We've taken a partial loss on a wagon, we're out four horses and our man's still laid up with a sprained back, all from that one accident."

"All right, say I supply you a guard with every wagon."

Once more Ives' head moved in a definite negative. "No. A guard's got nothin' to do with a road caving in. We've got plenty of other business. Why run chances?"

Tom Kimbrell breathed a long sigh. "Any idea who'd have it in for you bad enough to have rigged that accident?"

"Not a one. Maybe whoever did it thought it would hurt you, keep you from getting your ties out. You've gone up fast, Kimbrell. Maybe there's a man or two around that doesn't like it."

"That could be," Kimbrell admitted with a spare smile. "Anyway, you're putting me in a spot, Cass. Would I be wasting breath to ask you again if you'd sell to me?"

"You would."

"I might go as high as fifteen thousand."

"No dice," Cass said mildly. Then he thought of something that prompted him to nod toward Bourke. "Besides, I wouldn't have all the say now. Rold here holds an option to buy Frank's half the business if it comes up for sale."

The bright gleam of anger at once flared in Kimbrell's eyes. He stared unbelievingly at Bourke. "How come?" he drawled.

Bourke shrugged. "I mentioned having a couple of things in mind, didn't I?"

Kimbrell's glance swivelled back to Cass. "How come?" he repeated.

"You wanted it all, Rold wanted only half," Cass said.

The look Tom Kimbrell gave him then was bitter, openly hostile. "Thanks, Cass," he said softly. "Thanks a lot."

Turning then without another word he nodded to Spohr and led the way out.

They crossed the outside platform and went down the steps and across to the tie-rail, neither speaking. Kimbrell unknotted his reins with a jerk that hurt the animal's mouth. It was then that Ben Spohr drawled, "Well, that takes care of that."

Kimbrell swung up into leather and started out ahead and as Ben caught up with him they rode the front line of the fence in silence, the anger visibly building higher in Kimbrell and Ben watching it.

They were turning the fence corner, headed for the foot

of the Spikebuck trail, when Ben finally asked, "You going to let him get away with it?"

"Let him!" Kimbrell's furious glance came around. "Just what the hell can I do?"

Ben lifted his heavy sloping shoulders, idly saying, "This Rold now. He's another like Ames. He'll hang on."

Kimbrell had nothing to say to that as their horses lazed along the line of the fence, drawing near the high shape of the barn's rear. It was then that Ben said almost pleadingly, "You goin' soft, Tom?"

Still Kimbrell didn't speak. When Ben saw he was getting no answer he shook his head in bafflement, sighing, "You been against setups like this before. Only before you did something about it."

His words brought a gradual, subtle change in Tom Kimbrell's expression as the anger written so plainly across his features gave way to a calculating look. Shortly he eyed Ben in a wondering, almost respectful way, drawling, "So I did, Ben. Thanks for reminding me."

Now his glance lifted and took in the barn as though noticing it for the first time. He said, "Hold on," and reined aside and over to a heap of refuse mounded against the base of the fence. He came out of the saddle there and reached out with a boot to kick a litter of empty tomato cans off one torn end of a discarded mattress. He reached down and ripped off the straw-stuffed corner of the mattress, Ben meanwhile watching with unfeined puzzlement.

Kimbrell stepped back into his saddle with that wad of straw and faded ticking in his hand. Not so much as glancing at Ben, he reached to the pocket of his vest for a match, thumbed the match alight and touched it to the straw.

When the straw was blazing nicely, he kneed his animal close in to the fence that here formed the barn's rear wall. He stood high in stirrup and it was a long reach for him. But finally he managed to push the straw up over the edge of the loft floor.

He lifted rein then and led the way unhurriedly on to the foot of the trail. Ben, coming in beside him, burst out, "Lord, I didn't mean a thing like that! The whole layout'll go!"

"Maybe," Kimbrell drawled lazily.

"And they'll know who did it!"

"Why would they? It'll take a while to catch. By that time we'll be long gone." Kimbrell eyed Ben coolly. "Now who's going soft?"

They stopped a quarter mile above, where the trail made a turning to hide the lower canyon, taking their last look below.

At first there was nothing to see. Then, very faintly, they made out a thin veil of blue smoke lazily lifting into the still air from under the barn's roof-peak.

Three

Dan Exin had taken his time on the drive from town, knowing there was no pressing need for his being at the yard until four, the earliest any of the wagons could be expected back from Canyon Line's various hauls that included runs from several tie camps down to Texas Creek, present center of the Rio Grande's activities. He was driving a light spring wagon well loaded with various and sundry items that had been collecting in the glutted Canon City freight warehouse for the past two weeks— several sets of mail order harness, some kegs of bolts and nails for Jim Manlove, a roll of heavy tarpaulin, a new set of crockery for Charley Wong, half a dozen salt-blocks and a lot of grub.

Since there was no place for the horses to go except along the road that snaked down the canyon alongside the new grade, Dan had been catching up on the news since leaving Texas Creek, many miles above. He sat leaning back against the seat, one boot on the brake, the other on a stack of Denver and Pueblo papers from which he now and then would exchange a finished issue for a fresh one. Every so often he would reach over to the reins wound about the seat brace, give them a yank and idly curse at the team, after which they would trot for perhaps a minute before settling back into their deliberate walk.

When the canyon widened and the yard came into sight the better part of a mile below, Dan regretfully folded his paper, put it with the rest and took the reins in hand. He didn't much care if Cass knew he had been loafing; but as foreman he made it a point to set a strictly businesslike example for the crew, something Frank Ames had insisted on. Idly now, as his glance ran over the yard, he was thinking that he missed Frank one hell of a lot. Frank had worked hard, played harder, and Dan knew that it would be many a moon before he ever drew wages for a man he liked half as well.

He saw the wagon standing at the far side of the blacksmith shanty and guessed it must be the wrecked one. He saw someone—Ira Gaines, probably—wheeling a barrow from the stables. He noticed a pair of riders out behind the barn along the foot of the Spikebuck trail and was faintly curious when they stopped there at the back of the barn. Then when they went on shortly he immediately forgot them.

He was real peaceful in his mind just now and presently found himself whistling a bar of *Marching Through Georgia*, keeping time with the off-gelding's hoof clop, wishing he hadn't been only a kid during the War his old man had so often talked about. That got him to wondering about the family. Sarah was near old enough to be getting herself a husband. He'd have to write and see how things were coming with—

He saw the smoke.

For one paralyzing second he thought his eyes were playing tricks, for there was nothing but that vapory haze hanging over the back of the barn's roof. Then suddenly he realized what he was seeing and lunged erect, leaning out and with rein ends slashing the team across hindquarters.

They jumped to a run so fast it drove him back onto the seat. He belted them time and again until they were running. He started yelling. He had shouted himself hoarse over the loud rattle of the lurching wagon before realizing he was too far from the yard to be heard. Then he groped frantically behind the seat for his carbine.

The shots panicked the team and they bolted. He dropped the carbine and had his hands full keeping the wagon in the road. When he saw Cass and someone he didn't know, a tall man, leave the office and look up toward him he stood up again, waving toward the barn yelling, "Fire! Fire!" so hard and loud it made his chest ache.

Cass came on beyond the fence corner and Dan could see him wheel and head for the barn at a run. Then the other man started running. The column of smoke from the barn's roof was thicker now, definite, turning a dirty grey. Dan saw Jim Manlove leave his shop and pound across the yard to disappear below the line of the fence. Then Dan took a chance, sawing the team off the road and down across the rolling, cedar-dotted slope toward the barn. Even though the geldings were at a full-out run he kept belting them with the reins.

He was maybe a hundred and fifty yards out from the barn—close enough to make out the stranger up there in the smoke pitching bales out of the loft—when one of the wheels hit a red ant mound, the tongue slewed around throwing the grey off stride and the wagon tilted up and over.

Dan dived from the arcing seat, lit hard on one shoulder and slammed into a chamisa bush. One second later he was on his feet, hearing Cass bawling, "Get an axe, Jim! Throw it up to him!"

Flames were leaping through the smoke up under the peak of the roof now as Dan ran in on Cass, who was pulling a blazing bale away from the fence. Dan's wind had been knocked out of him and his chest was heaving. Cass saw him coming and called something he couldn't even hear.

Then he pulled up winded alongside Cass, who roughly shoved him by one shoulder, saying, "Quick! Get up there and help Rold. He's cutting off this end there at the second upright."

"Why don't he throw the damn' stuff down?" Dan gasped.

"From that furnace?" Cass snapped. He was wild-eyed, panicked, and now lunged over to roll clear of the fence another of the blazing bales Bourke had pushed from the loft.

Dan climbed the fence, dropped aground inside it and ran for the outside ladder leading to the loft. He heard the sound of an axe ringing overhead and, looking up there, saw this stranger climb through a hole halfway up the line of the roof. As he watched, Bourke scrambled up to the roof-peak and began chopping the shingles away there.

Suddenly Jim Manlove rounded the end of the barn at a hard run. He was carrying an axe. At sight of Dan he stopped short and threw the axe in to the foot of the ladder, bawling, "Get up there and help! I'll bring the team around."

Dan picked up the axe and climbed the ladder fast as he could make his legs work. He saw it now, saw how they might save the barn by cutting off its blazing end and pulling it free of the rest of the building. *But there's damn' little time!* was his thought then, for he could already hear the roar of the flames, the heat rattling the cedar shingles as though a pair of colts were up there trotting along the roof.

He stopped at the head of the ladder and got to work with his axe on the foot-thick beam of the loft floor, cutting it close to the second upright. Between the strokes of his axe he could catch the heavier thud of Bourke's from overhead. When his blade bit through the beam he turned and started climbing up over the bales, out of breath and at once beginning to cough against the acrid bite of the trapped smoke. He knew exactly what to do now, seeing overhead a narrow slit of light shining along the sheathing where the stranger was hacking his way down the roof's far slope.

He wouldn't waste time climbing out onto the roof, he decided, but would chop the sheathing boards from underneath, down this other side. When he was halfway up the mound under the roof-peak he glanced off toward the blaze. A red curtain of flames stiffened him in quick panic. Then suddenly he was gagging and coughing against the bite of the thick smoke.

He didn't want to breathe but had to. Now as the panic built more strongly in him he saw his mistake. A man couldn't live breathing this smoke and heat. The fiery breath of the flames struck him as though he were standing close to the open door of a sawmill boiler. Frantically, he clawed his way up over the last two rows of bales, intending to reach the hole Bourke had made cutting the ridge pole.

A choked sob escaped him as he pulled himself up onto the highest bale. He gagged for a breath once more but it only brought on a racking cough. Now he saw that the hole wasn't big enough to let him through and, fear striking through him more strongly now, he went flat on his belly and rolled down out of the smother of heat and smoke. Quite suddenly a weakness hit him. His hand balled his shirtfront together and ripped it to the waist in a vain effort to ease the constriction of his lungs. He tried to drag himself over to the edge of this layer of bales, couldn't find the strength to do it. Then he shouted. But his croaking was only a whisper over the mighty roar of the flames.

From a great distance he could hear the jingling of a chain and the hoof-thud of trotting horses and he thought, *Hurry, Jim, hurry!*

That was the last he knew.

When the blade of his axe finally swung through the beam close above the eaves on that far side, Bourke turned and wearily climbed back up the slope, wondering, *Why don't they send up some help?* His shoulders and arms ached, his hands were raw with blisters and he wanted nothing so much as just one deep lungful of untainted air.

He was half doubled over by a racking cough as he gained the roof's ridge and paused there a moment, blinking against the eye-smart of the smoke to look below. There were others down there now with Cass Ives. Cass himself, along with another man, was straining against a length of wrist-thick chain that arced up to one corner of the barn's blazing end. Beyond Cass a thickset man squatted behind a team of horses hooking the chain to a singletree.

A sudden gust of smoke pouring through the hole where the chewed ends of the ridge-pole showed warned Bourke that time was running out on him. He lifted the axe and put all the supple strength of his ropy-muscled shoulders and arms behind the swing. The blade went through shingles and sheathing with that single stroke and he went on that way, backing a quarter-stride each time he raised the axe, cursing softly now and again when a swing would fail to bite through a board.

He became so absorbed in what he was doing, in wasting not a single ounce of his fast giving-out energy, that he came close to backing off the roof's edge at the bottom of the slope. When he caught himself, when he realized how nearly through he was, he began on the eaves beam with vicious fast swings.

Halfway through it he paused to call, "Pull it away!"

Through the fog of smoke he saw Cass lift his hand, saw the man with the team whip them into motion. Remotely, he heard Cass call, "What's happened to Dan?" But the words meant nothing to him as he lifted the axe again.

He felt the roof sway beneath him and jumped back as the half-cut beam cracked under his feet. The blazing end of the roof swayed out, swayed back again. A geyser of flame suddenly billowed out the gaping hole along the ridge and he climbed up there to kick loose several flaming shingles, loudly calling, "Hurry it!"

Down below Jim Manlove picked up a handful of gravel, threw it at the team, then swung his reins across their rumps. The two quarter-Morgans lunged against the harness, the climbing line of the chain came taut, the blazing end of the barn swayed out again.

Slowly, stubbornly, the whole flaming mass tilted outward. Suddenly bales commenced falling from the loft, thudding aground beyond the fence and thickening the huge column of smoke there. And now a sheet of fire shot twenty feet skyward as, with a creaking and a groaning of timbers, the barn end toppled over.

They all heard Bourke call stridently, "There's a man down there!" and it was Cass who was the first to understand, who ran in close to the flaming pyre and through the gap in the fence.

Charley Wong, his pale ochre face showing a mixture of fright and concern, followed Cass closely. Two of the four Rio Grande men who had run up from De Remer's tent camp came next and as they began helping Cass lift away the bales that had spilled out of the unburned end of the loft one of these asked worriedly, "How can he be alive?"

They uncovered one of Dan Exin's legs finally and it was Cass who said softly, prayerfully, "Easy now!"

While the Chinaman gingerly lifted the ninety-pound bale that was pinning Dan by the waist, the other three dragged him clear and then took him in their arms and carried him on around the barn and over to the bunkhouse. After a closer look at Dan's blackened face, at the tatters of his shirt hanging from blistered shoulders, Cass said urgently, "Charley, tell Jim to saddle the grey and kill her if he has to gettin' in to Canon! He's to bring back the doctor."

Yesterday patients had stayed away because of the wreath hanging on the front door. But today it was different. Kate hadn't wanted that grim reminder calling such callous attention to her grief, so this morning after Tom Kimbrell had left she had taken it down and thrown it in the alley ash-barrel. Not twenty minutes later it all started.

First came a Mexican grade worker with a carbuncle that badly needed lancing. Kate had made him drink half a glass of whiskey before using the knife. He fainted dead away and while he lay there unconscious she did a thorough job of it, even finishing the bandaging before she dampened a wad of gauze with spirits of ammonia and brought him around. He was sitting there in one of the office chairs, looking pale and shaken, when Edna Murphy burst in with the news that her mother was in labor.

Mrs. Murphy gave birth to a strapping ten pound boy just past one o'clock. Afterward, when the woman was comfortable, Kate crossed the Murphy's muddy back yard taking a short-cut to her own. She was halfway through her late meal when she heard the side door slam and went along the hallway to look into the office and say, "Would you mind waiting for ten more minutes? I—"

She really saw the patient then and knew at once that he couldn't wait those ten minutes. He was holding a bandana to his mouth, but that didn't keep Kate from seeing the way his nose was flattened to one side, nor did it hide the blood dripping from his chin.

"Horse kicked me square and fair," the man mumbled. And Kate at once forgot her half-finished meal and went to work on him.

There was a lull along about three and she went to the kitchen once more, washed the dishes and made herself some tea, now quite seriously wondering how she would set about finding the town another doctor. She was taking her first sip of the tea when someone else entered the office. She took the tea and a plate of sugar cookies with her in there.

Young Fred Brodie was with his mother, sniffling, his face flushed and eyes red with a fever. It took both Kate and Mrs. Brodie, between them, to get the youngster to swallow two tablespoonfuls of castor oil. Before they had finished old Arthur Grimes sidled in the door and sank heavily into the rocker, hanging his cane from its back and groaning a little as the chair took his weight. There was nothing she could do for him, Kate knew; only the coming of summer and warm sun could ease the complaint of his arthritis. Still, he had often seemed to improve when her father gave him those harmless sugar pills, so now Kate sent him limping away with a fresh box of them in his coat pocket.

She didn't quite have the door closed when Jim Manlove ran down the gravelled walk, nearly collided with old Grimes, then rushed up to the door saying breathlessly, "Miss, we need the doctor awful bad. Out at Spikebuck. Man's been burned. Busted up some too, how bad we don't know. Your father'll have to ride instead of using the buggy."

Kate couldn't think straight for a moment and stood there just staring at the burly blacksmith. Then she said quietly, "You haven't heard. Dad passed away early this week."

She saw a stricken look cross Manlove's broad face, saw the hurt and the shock of what this meant mirrored in his dark eyes. It made her say quickly, "But I've helped Dad a lot. I can come."

"You can?" he breathed relievedly. Then his look became worried once more. "It'd be a hard trip, Miss. We'd have to go down Spikebuck. Otherwise we might be too late."

"If it's that serious we're wasting time talking about it," Kate told him. "Go to the livery and tell Ralph to put my saddle on the roan. I'll try to be ready by the time you're back."

She changed to her blue-edged grey riding habit, thought about a hat and decided not to wear one. At the last minute she remembered how much colder it would be tonight and went to her room for her short quilted jacket. By the time Jim ran his horses around the corner above she was waiting on the porch, her father's small black satchel under one arm.

As Jim helped her up onto the side-saddle he apologized, "Wouldn't bother you if there was another doctor within thirty miles, Miss."

"You're not bothering me," Kate told him, and he seemed relieved.

Starting off down the street he led her roan by a length and kept looking back until she finally said, "We could go faster."

The look he gave her was grateful and at once he kicked the grey to an easy lope. Kate eyed the animal's wet flanks and was about to speak to him, to ask if the grey could stand the ride back. Then she decided that this man must know what he was doing.

As it turned out, Jim Manlove hadn't been at all sure of what he was doing. To save time he hadn't changed to a fresh horse, thinking the tired grey could keep up with the slow pace they'd naturally have to take on the girl's account. When he finally understood that Kate could ride as well as most men it was too late to do anything about it. So he took his chance, wanting to make fast time, and pushed the grey hard. As a consequence the animal played out shortly beyond the turn-off down Spikebuck at sundown. After that they could do no better than a steady jog.

This delay was why Bourke and Cass were waiting at the fence corner beyond the yard gate and peering so anxiously into the thickening shadows up Spikebuck when the hoof-echo of the two animals reached down to them nearly one hour later. They had been sitting on the office steps since the evening meal, Cass's impatience wearing thinner by the minute. Now, listening to the sounds shuttling out from the foot of the trail, Cass took out his watch and muttered, "Five hours already. If it isn't Jim, Dan's as good as gone."

"Don't be too sure about that," Bourke said quietly. "Far as I can see he's no worse."

They stood staring beyond the still-smoldering ruin of the barn's capsized end, the strengthening cadence of these oncoming riders rising over sounds shuttling from the yard where Ira Gaines and a driver were unhitching one of the high-bodied wagons just back from Texas Creek. Downcanyon the shapes of De Remer's guard tents glowed ghostily with lantern light and the talk of the men there drifted faintly out across the stillness.

Watching Cass now as the hoof-strikes came plainer, Bourke was strongly reminded of an undersized Ulysses Grant. Cass had the same stocky build, the beard was a lot like Grant's, so was the angle of the cigar jutting from Cass's mouth. Bourke's impulse from the beginning had been to trust this man, to take him into his confidence and tell him who he was. Yet he wanted to be sure, very sure that nothing had come between Cass and his partner that could even indirectly have been responsible for Frank's death. He supposed he was being too stubborn about it and, thinking this, was reminded of Eleanor, of her accusing him of mulishness; and he felt a faint annoyance blended with his wish that he could be in Canon tonight seeing her.

The indistinct shapes of a pair of riders abruptly came up out of the gloom. At sight of them Cass caught his breath, said explosively, "Hell, one's a woman! Can't be Jim after all."

A moment later Bourke was recognizing that slender, erect shape sitting the side-saddle of the animal following Jim Manlove's grey. "Did he go in after Doc Banks?"

"Who else? Banks is all there is."

"Didn't know that," Bourke drawled, adding, "This is his daughter. They buried her father yesterday."

Cass's head jerked around. "Mark Banks dead? How?" When Bourke simply shrugged, his glance still on Kate,

Cass said wearily, "Out here we never know what goes on."

Jim Manlove saw them now and came on ahead to tell them in hushed and urgent tones, "She's the best I could do, Cass. Her—"

"I know, I know," Cass interrupted irritably. He stepped on past Jim's horse then and as Kate rode up said courteously, gravely, "We're thankful you could come, Miss Banks. A terrible thing about your father. Sorry to hear it."

"Thank you." Kate's glance moved on to Bourke and even in this faint light he saw her stiffen with surprise. She said pleasantly, "Good evening, Captain," not waiting for his answer before she asked, "Are we in time?"

"Let's hope so," Cass said. "You'd better come straight on in." He turned to the gate and led the way across there, Jim Manlove walking his horse beside him.

Kate made no move to follow, letting her horse stand as she looked down at Bourke. "This man was full of the things some tall stranger had done to save the yard," she said. "So you're the one."

"We had some luck," Bourke admitted, wondering how he could have been so preoccupied last night as not to have noticed her striking looks. Tonight she seemed a different person, more alive and friendly.

"It was more than luck, Captain," Kate said. "Have you had as much with your own affairs?"

"None at all."

Abruptly now she held out the reins to him and, as he took them, laughed softly, saying, "You'll have to help me down. This has been more of the saddle than I like at one time."

She was completely at her ease when, reaching down to him, she let him take a hold beneath her shoulders and swing her lightly aground. For a moment as she steadied herself she clung to him and they stood quite close; and in that moment Bourke was powerfully aware of her, of her tallness and litheness and grace. Faintly he caught the scent of roses in her hair and when she looked up, asking, "Is this man badly hurt?" her expression was somehow so trusting and intimate, that he had to force his attention to what she was saying.

"Some bad burns," he told her, starting out beside her

now and leading the horse. "He must have taken a bad jolt on the head. Been out ever since."

"Is his breathing uneven?"

"Steady. Like he's sleeping."

"That's good."

Cass, waiting there by the gate for them, said as they approached, "Jim's going to clear the boys out of the bunkhouse. You'll have the place to yourself tonight, Miss."

"We'll see," Kate told him. "I should be back if it can be managed. The first of a whole crop of babies arrived today. They have a habit of picking a time when a doctor's away."

"Then we'll get you back as soon as we can." Cass added worriedly, "Only Dan isn't so good."

"Of course I'll not leave until he's out of danger." Kate's words brought a sigh of relief from him.

Bourke left them at the bunkhouse, offering to take the horses on over to the corral. Coming back again several minutes later he looked in to see Kate in a chair alongside Dan's bunk, Cass and Jim Manlove standing beyond her. Bourke didn't go in, preferring instead to remain there beyond the reach of lamplight quietly studying the girl, trying to puzzle out the answer to the changes he saw in her.

Those changes were quite definite. Her face, even in its serious repose now as she worked over the unconscious man, held no trace of that lifelessness he had found so pronounced on it last night. Once when she looked up at Cass and said something in a voice too low for Bourke to make out he noticed a clear-cut alertness, a vivacious fluidity in her expression that was almost startling. He was unable to define that quality to her looks that gave him the impression of seeing more of beauty in her than prettiness. Her finely moulded features were delicate, yet their strength was more pronounced than the delicacy. Tonight her eyes seemed brighter, a deeper green than he remembered—they made him think of a dark highly polished turquoise he had once seen set in a Navajo silver bracelet. He found himself waiting for her to speak again, wanting to hear the softness and richness of her voice. And now he also noticed the difference in the way she had done her hair, the deep coppery braids circling her head high in the front contrasting strongly with her severe, tight coiffure of last night.

When he finally realized he was eavesdropping and turned out across the yard, he was for the first time aware of how increased was his strong interest in this girl; and it irritated him immediately. That irritation was based on the same impatience he felt over having let himself become so involved with Cass Ives and the affairs of Canyon Line. Until this afternoon his loyalties and his purpose in being here had been unmistakable; Eleanor was the one woman who had ever deeply stirred him, hunting down Frank's killer was his one immediate concern. Yet here he found his interest not wholly on Eleanor and he had willingly taken certain risks this afternoon that hadn't even remotely helped him unravel the mystery surrounding Frank's death.

Just now he heard a heavy step crossing the bunkroom and looked off there in time to see Jim Manlove's wide shape move out the lighted door and head for the nearby cook-shack.

"Need any help?" he called.

"Just after some of Charley's clean towels," the blacksmith answered. "Everything's comin' fine."

Bourke watched the blacksmith enter the shack and presently return to the bunkhouse. For a time he listened idly to the low run of voices sounding from the stables where the crew waited for news of Dan, their shapes silhouetted by a lantern's feeble glow beyond the arc of a wagon's high wheel. Then, reluctantly, his thoughts turned back into their restive channel of several minutes ago.

He was rationalizing now, reasoning that there on the roof of the barn he had after all been trying to save something that was Frank's. Still, he was honest enough to admit that he hadn't once thought of Frank in connection with the yard's threatened destruction. He supposed he had simply wanted to be helping Cass, for there in the office with Kimbrell he had admired Cass's handling of an obviously ticklish situation, had respected the man's quick thinking and downright guts. Later, talking to Cass, he had learned that a stubborn loyalty to Frank's wishes had been the main thing backing the refusal of Kimbrell's offer. "For it was a plenty big chunk of cash he named," was how Cass had put it.

So now Bourke's thinking was oddly confused. Looking to the future he was strongly tempted to make good those half-truths he had used today in approaching Cass. He would enjoy being in a business like this, probably enjoy it as much as Cass and Frank had. He knew he could get along with Frank's partner, knew there was money enough in the business to make them both comfortable.

But then suddenly this pleasing run of his thoughts hauled up short as he remembered Eleanor, knowing the demands she would make of him in the years to come. Strangely enough the close-knit society of an Army post seemed to satisfy her. But, lacking that, she would want to live in a city, to have countless friends and a variety of entertainment. And Canon City offered blessed little of either that would be to her choosing.

That mood of last night, that same feeling of frustration and helplessness and important anger, was beginning to settle heavily through him now when a sharp call, "Rold!" cut in on his thoughts and brought him wheeling around to see Cass Ives standing in the bunkhouse doorway.

"Here," he answered, and Cass immediately started toward him.

Cass was several strides away when suddenly he began swearing—a strident, low-voiced cursing that had all the venom in it the small man could command. He came up to Bourke, went silent a moment, then all at once took the cigar from his mouth, tore it savagely in two and hurled it aground as though trying to break apart its ends. Then:

"By God, I'll kill him! Kill him, do you hear, Rold? Dan saw it all, saw him out back there reaching up to the loft! Right in plain daylight. The confounded gall of it! Why, he—"

Now, as Cass ran out of words and breath, Bourke had the chance to ask, "Who, Cass? Who?"

"Kimbrell! Who the hell else?"

"Dan's come around?"

"Enough to talk. Do you get it, Rold? Tom Kimbrell

tried to ruin me, wipe me out!" His face contorted with rage, Cass began cursing again, pacing beyond Bourke then wheeling back again.

"What you're trying to say is that Kimbrell set the fire? That Dan saw him do it?"

"What the hell else would I be trying to say! Dan was up the road there, saw it all. Why in the name of good Lord didn't I listen to Frank? He had the devil pegged from the first. How he was behind those fires that hit the tie-camps, the brawls that crippled their crews. Now he owns every damned last mill that cuts ties!"

"This isn't a tie-camp, Cass."

"No! It's more than that. It's what lets him get his lumber to a market. God A'mighty, don't you see it, Rold? Once this layout is his he can call his turn on prices. There's no other outfit in the hills to haul in ties against him."

"But he tried to wipe you out, Cass, not drive you out."

"Sure. Because he couldn't buy. With me out of the way he'd bring in his own wagons, have things his own sweet way."

Oddly now, a keen relief was crowding Bourke, a feeling that after all the day's happenings made sense. There was another thing, too, that made him drawl, "Cass, there's something I haven't told you."

"Let it wait!" Cass snapped. He slammed one knotted fist into his other open palm. "What have I ever done to him except own something he wants to hog? How the devil can a man even a score like this?"

"Shouldn't be hard," Bourke said.

"How?" Cass's head tilted sharply up.

"He's got a headquarters, a camp somewhere. Where is it?"

"Upriver, between here and Texas Creek."

"A timber yard?"

"A big one."

"Well, it'll burn, won't it?" Bourke drawled.

Cass's eyes came wide open with wonder. A subtle change rode through him; he was all at once calm as he breathed, "Now that's a thought!"

He turned quickly away now, starting toward the corral and saying brusquely, "This is something I'll handle on my own."

"I'll come along."

"No."

Bourke started out after him. "I had something to tell you."

"Save it. I'll be back in a couple hours."

"You'd better have it now," Bourke said, adding deliberately, "Cass, I'm Frank's brother."

"What about—" Cass stopped so abruptly Bourke nearly collided with him. "How's that?"

"I'm Frank's brother."

Cass was baffled, still angry. "Look, Rold," he said tartly, "I'm too riled to think straight. What you say doesn't make sense with your name."

Bourke nodded. "Ames was my mother's maiden name. Frank may have had his reasons for using it. I wouldn't know." He waited and, when Cass didn't speak, asked, "Didn't Frank ever mention having a brother in the Army?"

"Come to think of it, he did," Cass said wonderingly.

Bourke poked his wide chest with a thumb. "I'm the one."

"Then why—"

When Cass hesitated, Bourke drawled, "Why do I come here with a put up story about wanting to buy into the outfit?" He smiled thinly, supplying his own answer, "Because I had to be sure of you."

"Sure of me how?"

"Frank was murdered, Cass."

"No!"

Bourke nodded. "Doc Banks wrote me about it. Not much, but enough to get me down here. Then Banks died before I could talk to him. So I'm looking around."

Cass heaved a deep sigh that ended in a low whistle. Things were happening too fast for him to take it all in and it was a long moment before he asked, "You're sure of this, Rold?"

"Very sure."

Now Cass shook his head, as though to clear his numbed senses. "Who would have wanted to kill him?"

"You know more about that than I could."

"No one I know of."

"Tom Kimbrell?"

"No, not Kimbrell. Frank saw Kimbrell only once that I know of. That was the first time he tried to buy us out. We all opened a bottle and everything was pleasant."

"Yet you say Frank turned him down."

"What of it? Does a man kill for a reason like that?"

Bourke drawled, "Okay, we forget Kimbrell. Except for this other. Do I get to side you?"

Cass gave a slow smile, saying in a clipped yet gentle way, "You do."

Tom Kimbrell took his table in the *McClure House* dining room that evening at the usual time, seven. The tables were crowded yet Kimbrell had one to himself, as usual. The waitress came at once to take his order, saying the usual pleasantries and finally asking, "Medium rare tonight, Mister Kimbrell?"

"Like it always is, Alice."

A dollar left beside his plate perhaps twice each week, plus an occasional side of beef delivered to the kitchen at his own expense, bought Tom Kimbrell promptness and privacy with his meals, along with far better fare than the ordinary run of hotel guests received. Tonight's meal was typical of the unattractive offerings—boiled beef, soggy dumplings, a watery variety of canned tomatoes, biscuits or bread, apple or apricot pie, coffee. Kimbrell had long ago learned to do better.

As soon as Alice left with his order Kimbrell let his attention unobtrusively stray to a neighboring table which was, oddly for the crowded room, also occupied by only one person. The girl there was strikingly pretty and dressed so fashionably that Kimbrell at once knew she must be straight from the East. And now as his interest came more strongly alive he was wishing he had taken the time to change to his grey suit rather than wear this black one out of press from half a day in the saddle.

Eleanor Hyde presently became aware of his regard

yet managed outwardly to ignore it completely. She had seen him come in and take a side table obviously reserved for him. His bigness and his rugged handsomeness had made their definite impression on her. But now, after making sure that he had noticed her, her interest in him gradually lagged before her growing irritation at Bourke's tardiness.

She was as out of sorts this evening as she had been since awakening in mid-afternoon. A walk along the street and an inspection of what the shops had to offer had been most disappointing. Having in that brief excursion seen all that interested her of the town, she had freshly resolved that she must persuade Bourke to leave. Thinking over what he had said this morning, she found it absurd. Somehow she was going to change his mind.

When the waitress promptly brought Kimbrell his meal she became even more impatient and annoyed. She had ordered several minutes before Kimbrell and a furtive glance at his plate showed her he was eating steak, an item that didn't appear on the menu. So when Alice left Kimbrell's table and passed her she asked coolly, "Must you keep me waiting?"

"In a minute, ma'am."

"Just a moment." Eleanor's sharp words stopped Alice as she was moving on. "I should like to change my order to steak. Rare if it's tender, well if it isn't."

"We don't have steak tonight, Miss."

Eleanor couldn't help glancing Kimbrell's way. She was about to protest but caught herself in time. Nothing was to be gained by making a scene, so she put all the iciness she could summon in her words as she said, "Very well then. But don't keep me here all evening."

Alice moved back the way she had come, past Kimbrell's table. Eleanor saw Kimbrell say something to the girl who turned back, leaning down to him. When he glanced Eleanor's way she looked quickly aside, realizing they must be talking about her. Then shortly Alice went on into the kitchen.

The minutes dragged on and when the waitress reappeared it was to serve a table at the far end of the room. Kimbrell finished his meal and left. Then finally Alice came from the kitchen with a crowded tray and carried it Eleanor's way.

"Sorry to make you wait," Alice said before Eleanor could word the reprimand she had prepared. She put Eleanor's plate before her. On it was a juicy steak. "Tom Kimbrell wanted you to have this."

Eleanor was confused, no longer angry. "Tom Kimbrell?"

"The gentleman that just left that side table, Miss. I had it cooked rare. It's tender. Mister Kimbrell always buys good meat."

Eleanor's look was one of polite surprise, although there was really none in her. "Will you thank him for me, please?"

"That I will, Miss."

It was a good steak, the best piece of meat Eleanor had eaten since leaving home. Regardless of her irritation with Bourke over having made her dine alone and unescorted she enjoyed her meal.

When she had finished and left her table to go out into the lobby it was to see Kimbrell sitting in one of the leather chairs by a street window half facing her. When his glance casually touched her and moved on she had the thought, *He's a gentleman, anyway, not like these others.*

She didn't bother to analyze the impulse that turned her toward his chair then; often she would do that, give way to an impulse without asking herself where it was leading her. So now she walked up to him, giving him that smile a mirror had many times told her was her most charming.

"Mister Kimbrell?" she asked as he finally noticed her and rose from the chair.

He grinned broadly, nodding. "Yes, I'm the one. When Alice said you tried to order steak I couldn't see her disappoint you."

"You have my thanks, Sir. It was very kind of you."

"Not at all. Out here we just try to be hospitable." He stepped aside, motioning to his chair and then pulling another over alongside it. "Would you care to sit here with me and watch the street? There's very little else to do this time of day."

"Or any time of day." Eleanor laughed lightly, then hesitated a proper moment before accepting the chair. "I can stay for just a minute," she told him. "I'm expecting someone."

"So?" he politely queried as he sat beside her. "Anyone I'd know?"

"Probably not. A man by the name of Bourke Rold. He's just come to town."

He straightened, not attempting to hide his quick interest. "Rold? Of course I know him. Met him last night." . . . She was never to know the irony behind the smile he gave her . . . "Fact is, I've made him a business proposition."

A look of alarm touched her blue eyes and before she quite realized it she was saying boldly, "Whatever it is, I trust Bourke won't take it. I'm hoping he'll leave with me in another day or two." She realized how he might miscontrue her words and added, "We're to be married."

He nodded graciously. "My compliments to you both. I must say that Rold has a way with him."

She eyed him now in a direct way, her thoughts quickly weighing an odd impulse. Then, as before, she was following her urge without quite thinking it through, saying, "I wonder if you could help me."

"If it's at all possible," he agreed politely.

She tried to look embarrassed. "It's that . . . well, I've already said I hope Bourke won't take whatever you're offering him. You see, it's that he shouldn't really be here."

"He shouldn't?"

Now she was determined to go through with it. This man wasn't as uncouth as most she had seen today and this chance of having a sympathetic listener was too tempting to be overlooked. She was worried about Bourke. Perhaps Tom Kimbrell really was the man to help her.

"No, he shouldn't," she told him, her mind made up. "Bourke has done a foolish thing, thrown away a fine career on a mere whim, a grudge. Last week he resigned a captaincy in the cavalry."

Kimbrell frowned. "A man doesn't do a thing like that without reason."

"Of course not. But Bourke's reason is at fault. He's here

with some fantastic idea of revenge. His brother died here recently. Bourke has foolishly decided there was something behind it. Murder, foul play, something."

"Who was the brother?" Kimbrell asked. There was an abrupt wariness in him that would have taken a sharper eye than Eleanor's to detect.

"A man by the name of Ames. Frank Ames. Did you know him?"

Once again his face set seriously to mask his real thoughts. "There's an Ames runs a freighting business somewhere up Leadville way."

"There was, you mean. He's the one. He was drowned. Bourke insists there was something behind it."

"And was there?"

Eleanor tossed her head impatiently. "Who's ever to know? Bourke has nothing to go on, nothing whatsoever. Yet he throws everything to the winds and comes down here on the barest chance of turning up something. I . . . I hardly know what to do. We were to have been married right away. Yet now he doesn't even know what he's to do when he's finished here." She gave him an appealing look, asking with unfeigned helplessness, "What would you do, Mister Kimbrell?"

He sat there eyeing her gravely a long moment and in the end lifted his heavy shoulders, telling her, "That's a tough one."

"I'm worried, very worried. Something has to happen before it's too late."

"Isn't it already too late?"

"No, it isn't. I haven't told you that my father is his commanding officer. Father's holding his resignation, hoping he'll come to his senses."

Kimbrell's look sharpened. "So you've somehow got to get him out of here and back . . . back to his duties before it's too late?"

Eleanor nodded mutely and Kimbrell eased down in his chair trying to think. Finally he gave her an oblique glance, drawling, "Rold has a mind of his own. It would take a lot to change it."

"I know."

He sat in silence for a considerable interval. Then abruptly he thought of something. "This means a lot to you?"

"Can't you tell it does?"

He tilted his head in a slow nod, wryly drawling, "I'd be working against my own interests in helping you. But I will."

Gladness touched her delicate features now and all at once she reached out and laid a hand on his arm. "Will you? Oh, if I only thought that between us we could do something!"

"Possibly we can." It was a long moment before he added, "We would have to trick him some way."

A faint alarm touched her glance, then gradually died. "Yes, I suppose that's the only way."

"You'd be willing to do that?"

"I would. Oh, I would! Anything!"

He nodded quite gravely, drawling, "Then give me the night to think about it."

The game at Kimbrell's tie camp usually began each evening as soon as the cook cleared away the dishes and tonight was no exception. Day before yesterday had been payday, with a consequence that by now most of the week's wages for the crew lay in two pockets rather than in the five it had originally occupied. And tonight Ben Spohr was here to make his contribution.

Or so it seemed at first, for Ben's cards ran poorly and in the first hour he dropped over forty dollars. But then his luck changed gradually; he came even, began winning a little.

Ben had just laid down a winning hand, a heart flush, and his thick arms were sweeping the money from the table's center when the cook's voice bawled from the kitchen:

"Fire!"

Ben Spohr's big frame stiffened. The eyes of every man at the table shuttled kitchenward.

It was Spohr, a second later, who caught the flickering rosy glow at the upriver window. He lunged erect, hurling his chair clear and running for the door with the others at his heels.

They jammed through the door and fanned out to either side of Ben, who came to a sudden halt. Then they, like he, stood dumbfounded by what they saw.

The sheer-climbing walls of the canyon were alight with a reflected glow. Three plumes of flame leaped high from the ranked piles of ties lining the road riverward. Beyond, two tents were already nothing but torches funnelling their blazing fragments skyward, the three remaining ones lighted from inside by an orange glow. And now from upriver another hungry tongue of flame licked against the blackness to mark a fresh blaze in a stack of bridge timbers newly delivered that day.

Spohr bellowed, "Get out there! Take axes, crowbars, anything to dump that stuff into the river!" He turned now and roughly shoved away the man nearest him.

He went rigid then, thinking of something. An instant later he was wheeling inside the shack and pounding into the kitchen. He reached down the Greener he had remembered always hung above the back door; he broke open the shotgun, checking the loads.

A look of rage patterned his unshaven face as he lunged out the door and over to the rail nearby where his horse stood head-up eyeing the flames riverward. The cinch hung loose but Spohr didn't give that a thought as he vaulted to the saddle. He savagely jerked the horse around and rammed home the spur and the animal went away at a run.

Behind him someone shouted his name. Ben paid no heed. Shortly he was in the deep shadows beyond the fires, downriver from them, but he rode another two hundred yards to a point where the canyon narrowed before viciously jerking the horse down out of its run.

He slid aground, looped reins about the horn and kicked the horse, sending him on down the road. His roving glance showed him a juniper growing close to the road's ruts and he ran over there and in behind the squat tree, breathing hard yet trying not to as he listened for a sound.

All he could hear was the distant shouts of the crew and the low roar of the fires. He squatted on one heel now, grounding the stock of the Greener and leaning heavily on the weapon as he peered into the flickering shadows toward the camp.

Ben Spohr was playing a hunch, a hunch based on that upriver fire at the bridge-timber stack having been the last to break out. Whoever had set that blaze wouldn't have had the chance to circle the camp and strike this lower stretch of road. And, if his guess was correct, this unknown man would be heading away from here downriver.

It was less than two minutes later when his hunch paid off. He saw the pair of riders drifting toward him, one a dwarfed shape in the saddle, the other a high one. He recognized them both as they walked their horses out of the trees to his right, close in to the base of the canyon wall. Then they were drifting toward the road, not hurrying, even stopping once to look back as they came down on him.

He plainly heard Cass Ives say, "Let's move. They'll be on the prowl." And Cass lifted his horse to a trot.

Ben let Ives go on past. It was the other man he wanted. And as he came slowly off his knees and moved around the far side of the bushy tree he was remembering the aching jar of Bourke's shoulder last night against his chin. Never before had anything hurt him quite like that.

He let Bourke walk his horse to within twenty feet of him. Then he cocked both hammers of the Greener. He stepped out into the road. There was plenty of light to make his target clear.

Bourke hadn't yet seen him, turned in the saddle as he was and peering back at the torches of the tie-stacks. But the horse saw Ben and came to a stand.

It was then that Bourke looked around.

Four

Bourke had that faint warning of the horse coming to a stand as he looked ahead. He saw Ben Spohr's thick shape there close before him. He saw the shotgun, the barrels agleam with the fire's reflected light.

Ever so slowly he laid his hands on the horn of the saddle, waiting. Spohr stood rock-still, the Greener's butt-plate within a hand-spread of his shoulder.

When after several seconds Spohr made no move, Bourke stopped holding his breath. "Guess I should have done a better job of it last night," he said.

He saw his words strike Spohr. The shotgun rocked into line. And now he was staring down its twin bores.

But nothing happened. Nothing. The seconds dragged on until Bourke could stand it no longer. "Would money make any difference?"

Spohr neither spoke nor moved. Bourke could catch the wicked gleam of the man's eyes. He was no longer afraid; but suddenly this waiting was too much for his nerves and he said, "Shoot if you're going to!" his voice bitter with anger.

Still Spohr only stood there, his stare unblinking and hateful.

Bourke understood something quite suddenly then. He had nothing to lose. Absolutely nothing. So he lifted rein and walked his horse obliquely on at Spohr. He came abreast the man, barely ten feet from him, no longer watching him although he could sense his turning. The muscles along his abdomen became so tight they ached. His mouth was dry with a salty taste and he could feel the beat of his heart along his neck.

Now Spohr was behind him and a tingling ran the length of his spine. He wanted to double over and rake the horse with spur. He didn't. He sat there too rigid against the sway of the leather under him.

He began wondering how far the horse had carried him beyond Spohr. Twenty feet? Thirty? He wanted to look back, didn't. And still the horse continued on at that steady walk. No sound came from behind.

Then he knew it was over. He was all at once so weak he had to grip the horn to keep from swaying. Very deliberately now he stopped his animal and looked back.

Spohr still stood there, boots planted wide but the shotgun hanging at his side now. The leaping fires upriver silhouetted him plainly. He was looking this way. Although the distance was too great—eighty yards perhaps—Bourke imagined he could still make out that enraged set of countenance he would long remember.

He wanted to lift a hand to Spohr. Or perhaps he wanted to call out to him. Instead he only turned and put the horse on at a trot, trying to think out Spohr's reasoning and getting nowhere.

Cass was waiting for him several hundred yards below at the bend in the road. As Bourke came up, Cass said delightedly, "Man, we called that turn! Look, even the river's ablaze. They're throwing the stuff in."

Dully, Bourke's glance went above. He saw the river's foaming width marked by blazing ties that were gradually swamped and guttered out as they raced down between the rocky banks. A bunch of ties and bigger timbers floated past close below, upending as they struck a rapids and sending a low thunder over the stream's steady roar. Above, the canyon was lighted brightly as by daylight, the fires leaping upward and funnelling sparks all the way to the rims. Yet Bourke was only half aware of all this, his thoughts still on Ben Spohr. He was trembling now with the easing off of the past two minutes' nerve strain.

"Cass," he said quietly, "Ben Spohr was back there."

"Good. Makes it all the better."

"But he was there by the road. After you went by. Had his chance at me."

It was several seconds before Cass said, "Then it couldn't have been Spohr you saw."

"It was. He let me go." Bourke slowly shook his head. "Remember that, Cass. He let me go."

There was something in his tone, in the gravity etched on his lean features, that made Cass say quietly, "I'll remember."

They were wordless as they rode on. They had taken many turnings along the deep-walled road before Cass finally ventured to speak. "Well, it was worth the ride, friend. He stands to lose a damn' sight more than we did."

After a long moment Bourke asked, "What comes now?"

Cass shrugged. "That's your say as well as mine."

Bourke thought about it. "I'd keep a man with a thirty-thirty out front and back at night," he said. "If we're still hauling for him, pull out and get our business elsewhere."

Cass chuckled softly. "Now you sound like Frank." More soberly he queried, "How sure are you about what happened to Frank?"

"There was Banks' letter. And Frank's, both hinting at the same thing."

Cass let the silence run on for perhaps a full minute before he drawled, "Come to think of it, Banks did have something to say at the inquest about there being no water in Frank's lungs or stomach. And there was a skull fracture. So we decided he'd probably taken a fall before the river got him."

"How could he?"

Cass shrugged. "It was at night, Frank was driving a light rig along a stretch of this road above here. He could have gone to sleep and fallen off the wagon any number of places where the road hangs over the water. Or he could have taken a spill climbing down the bank for a drink, say."

"Could have, yes. But Banks had another idea."

"Mark could have been wrong, Bourke."

"Sure," Bourke admitted. "But was he? Cass, this thing's got to the point where I'm even wondering if maybe Banks didn't take his fall so he'd never get to tell what he knew about Frank."

"Now it's you that's wrong," Cass said. "The girl seemed to want to talk about it. According to her, Mark was in plain sight of a rail crew up the Gorge that day. Two of them saw it happen. Some rotten rock gave way under him."

"Why was he up there?"

"Climbing. It was his way of lettin' off steam, like you or I would take to drink or cards, say. He'd go out and climb whenever his patients would let him, which wasn't too often. It was a game he picked up twenty or thirty years back, across in the old country when he was studying medicine. He was too old for it and it finally got him."

"At just the wrong time for me," Bourke said in a dry way. Then he thought of something else. "Does the girl think Dan will pull through?"

"Easy, she says."

"Then she's going back tonight?"

"Wants to. Jim can take her the long way 'round."

"Better let me save him the trouble. I should be in town."

"Running down something on Frank?" Cass shook his head. "You'll not find a thing. Frank had more friends than a man could count. And no enemies. Unless—"

"Unless what?"

"Unless someone he knew before he came here caught up with him."

Bourke considered that, saying finally, "No. He'd have mentioned it in his letter."

"Then we're guessin' blind," Cass drawled, and from then on they took the road at a faster pace, sighting the pinpoint gleaming of the yard's lights well below them some thirty minutes later.

They found Dan asleep and all of the crew but Jim Manlove already turned in, having taken their blankets to the barn. Kate wanted to go back to Canon tonight and it was decided Bourke should take her. She left a jar of salve and a sedative for them to give Dan if he had trouble sleeping. When Cass finally helped her up onto the buckboard seat beside Bourke, opening a blanket and spreading it over her knees, she made the offer of riding out tomorrow to change Dan's bandages.

"Wouldn't hear of it," Cass told her. "Unless he has a turn for the worse you've lost yourself a patient. Miss Banks, I'm ashamed of your charging only that one dollar. It was worth twenty to have you here."

"Dad's many times travelled further than this for his dollar," she said, adding, "Good night," as Bourke lifted the reins.

The buckboard was beyond the fence and the team settling into a walk up the long grade down which Dan had raced his wagon this afternoon before either of them spoke. Then it was Kate who said, "So you're in business."

"Whether I like it or not." Bourke grinned with a wry expression she could barely make out in the starlight.

"The men will like it, Captain. And you're lucky to have that nice little man as a partner. I like him. He reminds me of those black cubs you see in the high country about this time of year. Only they don't have his temper."

Bourke knew she was thinking of Cass's outburst there in the yard earlier and said nothing; and presently she was looking up at him to ask, "You don't believe Exin's story, do you?"

He took his time answering that, finally drawling, "Does it matter what I think?"

"Yes. I'd like to know."

"Then I believe it."

She drew away on the seat and he could make out the stubborn set of her features as she asked, "That Tom Kimbrell would stoop to such a thing as setting that fire?"

Bourke shrugged. "He had a reason."

"What reason?"

"He's been wanting to buy the yard. Cass and Frank wouldn't sell."

"That's not reason enough!"

"Not alone, no." And Bourke went on to tell her of Cass's theory of Kimbrell wanting a monopoly on the tie business.

She listened without interrupting, waiting until he had finished before saying with a low-voiced intensity, "I'll never believe it! Tom is a gentleman. He's made his money honestly. You haven't a shred of proof in what you're saying."

Bourke wondered what she'd think of the Rio Grande having hired him to watch Kimbrell as he drawled, "Let's get off Tom Kimbrell. See how the Dipper's tipped around. Must be past eleven."

"I don't care if it's noon! You're being unfair to Tom! Next you'll be saying he killed your brother."

"No," Bourke drawled seriously. "I won't be saying that." He was telling the truth. Frank's death didn't even remotely enter into what had happened today.

Now she edged even further away along the seat but a moment later evidently realized how childish her action was, for she moved back again. And presently she said, "Let's be fair to Tom. In the first place, Exin admitted he was about where we are now when he saw Tom. Take a good look back. How far is it?"

Bourke looked around. There was only one lamp burning far below in the yard, its pinpoint gleam so small

Bourke couldn't decide whether it came from bunkhouse or cook-shack window. "Better than a mile," he admitted.

"Closer to two. Could you recognize Tom Kimbrell at this distance?"

"Probably not."

"Then Exin could be wrong."

Bourke was remembering the time element now, how closely Dan's shots had followed Kimbrell's and Spohr's leaving the office. But he wasn't adding any coals to the blaze of Kate Banks' anger, so he said mildly, with a low chuckle, "All right, he's wrong." He was glad that neither he nor Cass had told her of the tie-camp fire.

"He has to be! You must understand that. I like Tom Kimbrell. He likes me well enough to have asked me to marry him. And I'm loyal to my friends."

Bourke gave her an oblique glance, the smile still easing the angular lines of his face. "And are you marrying him?"

Her look shuttled away. "Whether or not I am has nothing to do with this, Captain."

She showed him a definite coolness now as she leaned against the seat-back, and for minutes that added finally to better than half an hour the steady rhythm of the team's rattling hooves was the only sound that broke the night's stillness. Presently Bourke felt the touch of her shoulder against his and looked around to see that she was nodding. He pulled the blanket up and gathered it close about her shoulders, hoping she would be asleep when they came to that stretch of road that ran through Kimbrell's tie-camp.

She was asleep, soundly, her head on his shoulder, when the rosy tinge of the dying tie-stack fires came up out of the canyon's shut-in blackness. She was sitting close against Bourke's right side, so close that there was a faint unease in him over how quickly he could reach his gun if it became necessary.

Coming in abreast the camp's mess-shack he had a bad moment. For as the team came up on the building the door opened to flood the road with an orange wash of lamplight, and a man with a carbine cradled in the crook of his arm stood there looking out. The buckboard rolled through the wedge of light, the man didn't move. Then the door slowly closed and Bourke knew he wasn't to be stopped.

The Texas Creek camp was deep in slumber as the buckboard rattled through it much later. The road turned rough for a long stretch as it climbed beyond and Kate stirred, suddenly coming wide awake and looking up at Bourke. Yet she didn't lift her head from his shoulder as she asked drowsily, "Arm asleep?"

"Not yet." He looked down at her, catching the fragrance of her hair and feeling an odd excitement in her complete trust of him.

"I'm so warm and comfortable," she murmured. "Tell me if you want me to move."

"I will."

Further on, he was sure she was asleep once more. He was therefore startled when she abruptly said, "I forgot to mention it, but using tobacco on those burns was the best thing that could have happened for Exin. Where did you hear of it?" She hadn't moved, hadn't lifted her head, and her voice was muffled against the sleeve of his coat.

"From the Snakes up in Idaho," he told her. "They grow all their medicine."

"You've fought the Indians?"

"Off and on."

She didn't speak again for several minutes. Then, so low that he could barely catch her words: "What is it about the Army that holds men the way it does?"

He had to think very deliberately before answering, realizing that no one had ever before put this question to him, that he hadn't really ever put it to himself. And finally he told her, "The uniform's part of it. You learn a respect for it, learn to look after it better than the civilian does his clothes. It's no finer or poorer than the next man's. So the man himself stands out for what he is."

"You would be very handsome in a uniform, Captain." Suddenly her head lifted from his shoulder. She was wide awake. "How can you be going into business if you're still in the Army?"

He tried to tell her, going as far back as her father's letter and Baxter Hyde's refusal to grant him leave. Then he had to mention Eleanor and before he quite realized it he was speaking of the many doubts that had been nagging him this past week, arguing the rights and wrongs of the decision he had made. When he became conscious that he was breaking a long habit of keeping his innermost thoughts strictly to himself, it was too late. She put a question or two and whatever reticence was in him thawed before the warmth of her straightforwardness and outright interest. The words came easily as he talked on. He found himself wanting her to understand why he had acted as he had; it seemed really important that she should.

"Yes," she said softly when he fell silent at last. "I think you were right. But Eleanor must be far different than you say. A woman will give up many things to help her man. You have your chance here. She'll want you to take it."

"You could be right," he drawled, not believing it and feeling a faint embarrassment over their discussing something so personal as his relations with Eleanor.

Now he was reluctant to say anything more and shortly she told him, "You're the kind that makes things come out right in the end, Bourke." And as she pulled the blanket more tightly about her and let her head go to his shoulder again he was inordinately pleased at her having called him by his given name.

The buckboard rolled along Canon City's Main Street just twenty minutes short of four that morning. The new moon was a thick orange sickle hanging over the far peaks of the Sangre de Cristos and Bourke's arm was around Kate as it had been the past hour to keep the blanket from working off her shoulders. There was a before-dawn wintry bite to the air and as he reined in the team before her house and gently shook her by the shoulder he could see his breath against the starlight.

She wakened like a child, rebelliously, softly protesting until Bourke, chuckling, drawled, "Kate, you're home."

She sat up then and slowly shook her head, looking about her with a growing awareness. He stepped aground and came around to her side, offering her a hand. As she climbed down she said in mock-petulance, "I was so warm." Then, with a sleepy smile, she added, "You put yourself to a lot of trouble for me. Thank you, Bourke. You needn't come in."

He waited there while she went up the walk and opened

the door. The shadows under the porch roof were too deep for him to be sure, but he thought she turned and looked back at him before she closed the door.

Going on down the street, really feeling his tiredness now, he had to smile at his regret that the drive was over.

Gretchen arrived by the nine o'clock local that morning and rode from the station to the hotel in the open-sided mud wagon with the legend *City Transfer* lettered on its door panel. Eleanor was delighted at seeing her, for the moment forgetting her irritation and concern over Bourke's unexplained absence. The two of them fussed over the largest trunk Gretchen had brought, unpacking dresses and suits that needed pressing and meantime talking as though they hadn't seen each other in two weeks rather than in just the two days.

It was directly after Gretchen had gone to the kitchen with an armload of clothes to see about using an iron that the knock came. Eleanor wanted to run to the door but for once restrained an impulse and took her time about crossing the room to open it. It was Bourke.

When he took her in his arms she turned her cheek to his kiss. "You've some explaining to do, Bourke."

"I know." His grin was sheepish, guilty. "Got caught up in the hills on business and didn't get back until almost daylight this morning." A light of eagerness betrayed itself in his glance as, his arm still around her, he led her toward the window. "Let's sit. I have something to tell you."

She couldn't understand his good spirits and was becoming quite annoyed by them as she took the chair and looked up at him to say, "It must be good news."

"It is." Before he spoke again he dipped a hand into his coat pocket and brought out his pipe, looking at her inquiringly. As she nodded that he might smoke she was noticing a difference in him this morning. He seemed more like the man she had known on the post summer before last, his look younger, more carefree, showing only a trace of the strong maturity that had been so pronounced in him yesterday morning.

As he packed his pipe he was looking not at her but at his hands. "Eleanor, I have something to say and I wish you'd hear me out before we discuss it. Agreed?"

"Yes, Bourke." She sensed by his approach to this thing that she wasn't going to like it. But it was her way to keep that premonition well hidden now.

"This business of Frank's," he began awkwardly. "It's quite an outfit. Well established and making real money. Ives, Frank's partner, is honest as they come, easy to get on with." The pipe packed, he lit it, paying it a particular attention and still not glancing Eleanor's way as he added, "Fact is, I've never seen a better opportunity for a man."

She saw the line he was taking now and halfway understood what was to come, hating it and yet saying quietly, "Yes, Bourke? Go on."

"Now you must understand what the opportunities are." A suppressed excitement robbed his voice of its smoothness. "Here are two railroads building through this country, having to haul all their materials and supplies into the hills by wagon. Tons and tons of everything from spikes to flour, rails to tin cups. For a couple of years this country'll be a freighter's paradise."

"And—?"

His eyes, dark and warm and alive in their excitement, shuttled around to her now. "Eleanor, Cass Ives needs a partner. We get on. I'd like to take over Frank's half of the business."

She managed somehow not to show him the dread, keen and deep-striking as a knife, that cut through her. "Is that all?" she asked quite calmly.

He was watching her closely, judging how she was taking what he had told her so far. She seemed perfectly serene, in fact quite attentive, and the picture of her sitting there so beautiful, so wholly desirable, brought his next words out in a rush.

"Don't you see it, Eleanor? It's our big chance. A few years here and we'll have nothing to worry about. Afterward we can travel, go abroad. You'd have everything, Eleanor, anything you'd ever want."

She was staring up at him in amazement, in a way that mistakenly made him read eagerness into her look. He turned away now, drawing deeply at the pipe, pacing to the other window and then turning to say, "We could rent a house here in town. I'd be back and forth a lot.

Every so often we could get up to Denver to kick our heels."

"So you've even though of that, of me," she said brittlely, exerting a definite strength of will to keep her expression composed, placid.

" 'Course I have," he went on, not noticing the tell-tale pallor that was thinning the coloring on her cheeks. "Stack it up against the regiment, Eleanor. Up there we'd have probably two more years of living in a log shack, blizzarded up in winter and the summers spent guarding those sodbusters on their way through to Oregon. Then there'd probably be a stretch at Leavenworth. Those damn' stone buildings, the raw winters and that summer heat a man can hardly breathe! Here we'd have everything we want."

It was an awkward interval before Eleanor murmured, "So you've remembered your career after all."

The emptiness of her tone was the first inkling he had of her real thoughts. He regarded her closely, warily now. "You don't approve?"

"It's hardly for me to say, Bourke."

"You're the only one who does have a say."

"No, your mind's made up."

"Only if you agree."

She turned from him, looking out the window; and he saw her knuckles go white as she cleanched her hands tightly in her lap.

He came on around the chair and in front of her, reaching down gently to tilt her chin up. "Look at me, Eleanor." He studied the hurt in her eyes and was shocked to see she was on the verge of tears. "What have I said?"

She moved her head aside, lowering her glance. "Nothing, Bourke. Nothing at all. It's just that I'll have to get used to the idea." Quite suddenly her mind was made up to something. She had forgotten a thing that could very possibly change all this—her talk with Tom Kimbrell last evening—and now it became all-important that she should show Bourke no more of her feelings. She must manage somehow to deceive him until she had seen Kimbrell.

So when she looked up at him once more she was smiling. "You're so full of surprises, Bourke," she said, almost lightly. "Yesterday you were after one thing, today it's something entirely different."

"When I saw you yesterday I didn't know what I do now."

She came up out of the chair and stood close to him. "You really want this, Bourke? You're sure you do?"

"Yes," he said gravely. "It's what I want. It's a real chance for us."

"Then it's what I want, dear."

His face lost its gravity, lighted with an enthusiasm she remembered having seen only once before in him—on the night he had asked her to marry him and she had accepted. He took her by the arms now, his fingers gripping so tightly that she winced. "You really mean that?"

"I do, Bourke. Really."

Suddenly his arms went around her and he lifted her and swung her about so sharply that she gave a small cry of alarm. Then he was laughing with a sheer delight so unsettling that she found herself joining in, but for the far different reason of fighting a sudden panic. "You'll cut me in two, Bourke! Put me down!"

"Ellie, we'll go to Denver and you can order a whole houseful of furniture!" As he let her go she resisted the urge to remind him that she had never liked his calling her that. "We'll have Cass and Jim and Dan, the whole crew, in to a house warming. People will say, 'There goes that beautiful Mrs. Rold. *The* Mrs. Rold, of course.' You'll have the town by the ear! You'll—"

All at once his hurried words broke off. He gave her a mischievous glance and without explaining it stepped on past her to reach his hat from the chair by the door.

"Where are you going, Bourke?"

"You'll know soon enough." He was smiling at his secret, at her anxiety.

Before she actually realized it he was gone and she knew as certainly as though he'd told her that he was on his way to look for a house.

A real panic hit her then, along with a fear that she had gone too far with her deception to make amends. That fear sent her running from the room and down the hallway to the kitchen. Somehow Gretchen must find this man Kimbrell and bring him here.

When Eleanor finally did see Kimbrell—it wasn't until mid-afternoon—she was saved the awkwardness of his knowing she had sent for him; for he had come straight from the upper canyon after looking over the damage caused by the fire at his camp. He was therefore far more interested in what Eleanor had last evening proposed than she was then to realize, knowing as he did of Bourke's part in the firing of the tie-camp.

He had sent the clerk to her room for her and she found him waiting in the lobby, seated in the same chair as last night. As he sighted her he rose and bowed in a way she had never expected from a Westerner. His manners were flawless as they took chairs and began talking. It wasn't his way—nor would it have been hers—to come straight to the point. So for several minutes she had to listen with nicely concealed impatience to his recital of certain developments in the railroad war. Whatever they were, Eleanor gathered they were important. The Supreme Court had passed some opinion favoring one—the Rio Grande, although she wasn't interested enough to note that—and some local judge had interpreted the opinion in such a way that things remained pretty much as they had been for the past several months, both roads laying track as fast as they could toward Leadville.

"By the way, your friend Rold was up the canyon yesterday," Kimbrell said finally.

"He was?" Eleanor's tone was bland, seeming only slightly interested.

Kimbrell's handsome face took on a frown. "I've been thinking about our discussion last night, Miss Hyde." He eyed her measuringly. "Anything we do would, of course, have to be in the strictest confidence."

"Naturally, Mister Kimbrell."

"The sheriff is a trustworthy man. He won't talk."

"The sheriff?" Eleanor sat straighter in the chair.

Kimbrell nodded. "Yes. Providing you approve my suggestion."

"And that is?"

"You say Rold has resigned his commission. Would he be carrying papers in proof of that?"

Eleanor thought a moment, at length emphatically shook her head. "I doubt it since Dad is holding his resignation. It hasn't yet been accepted."

"So I reasoned," he drawled, leaning forward now with elbows on knees, lowering his voice as he continued, "This is what could be done. Any sheriff is always interested in picking up Army deserters. Now we could—"

"But Bourke's no deserter!" Eleanor got that far before she sensed part of what was coming and added quietly, "Excuse me. I should have let you finish."

"No, Rold's no deserter," Kimbrell said. "But can he prove it? Suppose I tell the sheriff this. Through my acquaintance with you I've learned by the merest chance that Rold is a deserter. You've somehow let that fact slip, although you're helping him in his pose as an officer who's resigned his commission. Now, rather than let Rold put up a defense when he's arrested, why don't we anticipate what he'd do?"

"What would he?" Eleanor was deeply interested now. She glanced beyond Kimbrell as a man strolled toward them from the desk, motioning Kimbrell to silence. She waited until the man had walked past and well out of hearing, then repeated, "What would he?"

"Send a telegram to his post, probably. Which is what we don't want him doing."

"So?"

"So, when I take my story to the sheriff, I suggest his wiring whatever Department of the Army Rold's post is in, asking if he has resigned."

Eleanor's look brightened. "And of course they'll say no, with Dad holding his resignation."

"Exactly." Kimbrell eased against the chair's soft back now, smiling sparely. "What do you think of it?"

"What . . . just what will they do with him?" Eleanor asked a trifle worriedly.

"I can even help there," Kimbrell said smoothly. "As a matter of fact, Sheriff Shaffer is away on business. There's a deputy in charge, a man of . . . well, shall we say a man of limited intelligence? He won't know exactly what to do.

I will. I'll suggest he take Rold across to Fort Garland at once."

"And where is Fort Garland?"

"Over San Luis way. Far enough so that Rold will be well out of sight. But here's something else. You'll have to help. You'll have to wire your father something of what we're doing. Maybe you can simply say that you've found a way of getting him back there. And you can ask your father to back the desertion story when Fort Garland communicates with him."

Eleanor was alarmed. "But won't we be getting Bourke into serious trouble?"

"Not if your father will help. Garland will take immediate steps to return Rold to his post. Once he's there it will be up to your father to take any action." . . . Kimbrell's smile broadened . . . "And I assume he'll see that his son-in-law's record is kept clean."

For almost a full minute now Eleanor sat without speaking, thinking of what Kimbrell had said, trying to see any flaws in his plan. Finally when she spoke it was in all seriousness: "If Bourke should ever learn that I've had anything to do with this he would hate me."

"He'll never know. If the thing kicks back you can always say I was lying in whatever I claim you told me." He nodded out across the lobby. "A few people may have seen us together and know we're acquainted. But they can't know what we've talked about, can they?"

"No," Eleanor murmured. "I suppose you're right."

He waited a long moment before asking, "Then I'm to go ahead with it?"

Eleanor gave him an odd, appraising glance. "Everything's quite clear, Mister Kimbrell, except for one thing. Why are you doing this for me?"

He chuckled softly. "I'm doing it for myself. Remember my telling you yesterday that I'd made Rold a business proposition?"

She nodded.

"Well, he took another. In a way he's becoming my competitor. Shall I put it that I've never before had the chance of removing competition and at the same time serving a lady?"

Slowly, Eleanor smiled. "You are very gallant. Then you'll go ahead with it?"

"If you say so."

"I do."

The late afternoon turned grey and warm, the clouds piling in against the distant Sangre de Cristos until finally, with the dusk, they hid the upper foothills and settled low over the town. The first big drops of rain were pelting the shingles of Tom Kimbrell's office-shack at his empty yard in town as he and Ben Spohr finished a somewhat lengthy and bitter talk.

"So you refuse to do it, Ben?"

"I do." Spohr's voice was toneless. He wasn't afraid of Kimbrell and his glance didn't drop away.

"I've been pretty good to you." Kimbrell's thumbs hung from the armholes of his vest and his boots were cocked on the desk corner as he leaned back in his chair blandly regarding his man.

"And I've earned my wages," Ben said flatly.

Kimbrell shrugged, took one hand from his vest long enough to wave it carelessly. "Okay. Bates will do it."

"Bates will do anything."

Kimbrell smiled a little. "So you have your principles, have you?"

"A few, yes."

"And what are they, Ben?"

Ben glowered down at him a long moment, not bothering to answer, then abruptly turned out through the open door.

His solid boot tread went fading down the walk as Kimbrell rose and went to the door to stand looking after him. Kimbrell noticed a certain doggedness in Ben's stride, in the way he walked head up and shoulders squared, paying no attention to the rain. And there was a real regret in Kimbrell as he thought then, *He was a good man.*

Presently, when Ben had turned the corner of the crossstreet below, Kimbrell took his poncho from a nail beside the door and walked back across his yard, calling, "Smitty!" He saw an old man in overalls come to the door of a shack that stood along the yard's back fence and walked over there to tell him, "Smitty, go on down and have a look around for Bates. Try the San Julian first. Tell him I want to see him." He reached to a pocket, took out a half-dollar and tossed it to the oldster, adding, "Don't spend this till you've found him."

"I won't, Tom."

Kimbrell idled there in the doorway of the shack several minutes after his yard man had gone, listening to the rain's steadying murmur, frowning as he gave his attention to a certain problem. Presently, buckling his slicker, he climbed through the rails of the back fence, cut across the vacant lot beyond and over to the next street. He went along it as far as the new brick courthouse. There was a light in the window of the sheriff's office.

When he entered the room it was to find Red Drury, the deputy, leaning across his desk hanging a bunch of keys from a wallpeg over the safe. When Red saw who it was, a harassed expression settled over his narrow face. Jerking a thumb toward the heavy bolt-studded jail door, he said without preliminary, "Well, he's in there. But, Tom, I swear to God I think he's talkin' gospel when he says he's no deserter."

"You know what the telegram said," Kimbrell drawled, smiling good-naturedly.

"Yeah. Only there could be some mistake."

"Not yours, Red. You didn't let on I was in on it, did you?"

"No. If he's asked once who tipped me off he's asked it a hundred times."

"Good. Let him ask. When do you take him across to Garland?"

"Tonight, soon as I eat. Lord, I hate that trip! It'll take two days."

"But save you a headache later. The old man would climb all over you if you let a thing like that go."

"So he would," the deputy said ruefully.

Kimbrell took off the slicker now, tossing it in the corner beyond the varnished roll-top desk. He offered Red a cigar, they both lit from the same match, and as Red sat on the desk Kimbrell started slowly pacing the length of the room and back again. Red watched him idly at first, then with a growing curiosity, finally to ask, "Something on your mind?"

"Guess there is." Kimbrell didn't break his stride. He would take four steps one way, swing slowly around and come back again. It was always just the four strides and Red got to counting them.

The deputy gave a small start as Kimbrell abruptly stopped and turned to him, drawling, "Red. I need your help."

"Anything you say." Red was somewhat flattered.

"Suppose," Kimbrell said, "you had a man working for you and you found out there was a dodger on him?"

"Dodger? Reward, you mean?"

Kimbrell nodded. "What would you do?"

"Hell, turn him in!"

"But suppose he was a man you'd hate to lose. A good worker, sober, a man to be trusted."

"Trust a man with a record?" Red drawled. "Hunh-uh!"

"But I have trusted him."

Red waited for him to go on and, when he didn't, asked, "Who is it, Tom?"

"Suppose I didn't turn him in," Kimbrell went on, ignoring the question. "The law would have something to say about that, wouldn't it?"

"Sure would."

Kimbrell looked down at his cigar now, using the stub of the match to trim the ash evenly. Then his glance lifted. "Okay. It's Ben."

Red Drury's glance widened with shock. "No!"

Kimbrell nodded glumly. "I'm probably a fool for telling you. But the thing's got me worried."

"What's he wanted for?"

"That's what you'll have to tell me. The way I get it, three or four men broke into a Wells-Fargo office in a town somewhere in New Mexico Territory. Ben was tangled up in it. It'd sure help if you could get me some word on it. Maybe it's not as bad for Ben as it sounds."

The deputy eased off the desk and turned to a big deal filing cabinet to pull open the middle drawer, drawling, "Shaffer saves every scrap of paper that comes to the office." He lifted out a bulging manila folder labelled *New Mex. Terr.* and brought it over to the desk, taking the chair there. "Any idea what year it was?"

"Not any. And if you don't find anything you're to forget I've said what I have."

Red nodded solemnly and began thumbing through the oddly assorted sheets in the file, some of them yellow with age. Within thirty seconds Kimbrell spotted the reward notice he was after, the one on Ben Spohr exactly like another in his box in the bank. But he let Red leaf on past it.

During the next ten minutes they found two notices on men whose descriptions closely fit Ben Spohr, Kimbrell nimbly rejecting each on the basis of some minor point. They finished going through the folder and Kimbrell drawled, "Not a thing." But Red wasn't satisfied and began again.

This time when he came to Ben's dodger the deputy caught it. When Kimbrell was sure of that, he idled on across the room, turned a chair backward and sat in it with arms folded across its back. Then Red was reading aloud, "Benjamin S. Madden, suspected of murder."

Suddenly the deputy's head lifted. "Here it is! Down here further it gives his middle name, Spohr."

"Just my luck," Kimbrell breathed disgustedly. He waved the hand that held the cigar. "Go ahead. What does it say?"

Laboriously, Drury read the notice aloud. Kimbrell only half listened, for he knew what it said almost by heart. When the deputy had finished, Kimbrell drawled, "Well?"

"It's him all right." Red was frowning now. "Only how'm I goin' to take care of him with this other on the fire?"

Kimbrell shrugged. "Your lookout, Red. Maybe Ben'll know something's in the wind and clear out before you're back from Garland."

"And maybe he won't! Tom, I'm going to leave it up to you."

"How?"

"You're going to hold him for me."

Kimbrell shook his head. "Not me."

"Look," Red said, "I hate to throw my weight around, but this is important. The old man would probably swear you in as a deputy and have you arrested for contempt or some such thing if you didn't do what he said. All I'm asking is that you hang onto Ben till I get back. If you can do it without his knowin', so much the better."

Kimbrell's glance went flinty. "Why should I do your work?"

"You know why, Tom," Red said worriedly, pleadingly. "Lord, I hate askin' it of you."

Rising now, Kimbrell stepped over and picked up his poncho, pulling it on as he drawled, "All right, I'll have a man watch Ben. But if he spooks and lights out he goes without my trying to stop him." He crossed over to the door, opened it. "You wouldn't want me to get a man killed doing your chores, would you?"

"No, I wouldn't," Red said seriously. "But there'll be hell to pay if he gets away. I'd lose my job."

"You could get another." Kimbrell stepped out, closing the door.

Red was worried and spent another twenty minutes finishing the cigar, which was a far better one than he was in the habit of smoking. At the end of that interval, when he went down the street through the rain to eat, his worry over what might happen to Ben Spohr while he was away had eased somewhat. That evening he ate a bigger and better meal than usual, thinking of the reward he stood a good chance of collecting on Spohr. He also spent twenty cents more than the county allowed for the meal he took back to the jail for his prisoner; for he liked Bourke and didn't like what he was having to do with him.

Sharply at eight o'clock one of Megrue's *Silver Cliff* stages, a Concord, splashed to the street's edge in front of the courthouse, the driver bawling Drury's name. And shortly the deputy and his prisoner, Bourke leading the way, ran out through the downpour and climbed aboard the coach, the driver calling down in a dry voice, "You order this rain just for me, Red?"

"Just for you, Sweetheart," Red answered.

He finished handcuffing Bourke to the outer brace of the

forward-facing seat alongside him as the driver booted off the brake and spoke to his two teams. The coach swayed into motion, gathering speed slowly with the horses wary of the slippery footing.

A cottonwood closely flanked the walk at the end of which the Concord had stood. Now a man who had been leaning idly out of sight behind the tree's thick trunk buckled up the collar of his poncho and sauntered away toward Main Street. The pale glow of the stage lanterns had let him see how Red Drury had handcuffed his prisoner to the seat. It was a thing he meant to keep in mind.

Some two hours after the stage had rumbled over the bridge and headed out the southwest road toward the Greenhorns, De Remer—who had come across to Canon this afternoon—heard about Bourke's arrest. When he was sure of his information he sent for the Rio Grande's telegraph operator, who presently walked up to the Main Street ticket office, unlocked, lit a lamp and went straight to his key to begin tapping out a coded message De Remer had given him addressed to William Palmer in Denver. The message said:

ROLD ARRESTED HERE AS DESERTER. AWAIT YOUR INSTRUCTIONS ON KIMBRELL SURVEILLANCE.

At about the time the telegrapher was turning out the lamp in the Rio Grande office, his message sent, Bourke was asking Red Drury, "How about me taking that other seat? I could use some sleep."

The rain laid a steady whisper of sound against the curtain Bourke had fastened on his side. Through Drury's window, open, shone the feeble glow of the lamp, enough light to let Bourke see Drury considering his question. And finally the deputy drawled, "Why not?" reaching for his Colt's first, then for the key.

Bourke hadn't especially wanted to take that opposite seat; he'd been hoping Drury would be careless and give him the chance he was looking for of making a break. Yet the deputy was anything but careless now. He handed Bourke the key and moved back into the corner, the .45

ready and aimed. So all Bourke could do was unlock the handcuffs, move to the opposite seat and fasten the steel bracelet to the brace there. Drury leaned over and tested the brace before he pocketed the key and then finally holstered the gun once more.

Bourke said idly, "You must be pretty hard up, doing all this to collect Army money. How much they paying on deserters now?"

Drury lifted his shoulders. "Haven't asked."

"There's seventy dollars in my wallet. Take it and turn me loose."

The deputy only smiled.

Bourke stretched out on the seat now, crooking his handcuffed arm so as to be comfortable. "Who turned me in?" he asked.

"That's twenty-two," Red drawled.

"Twenty-two what?"

"Times you've asked me that since we climbed in here."

"Well, how about an answer?"

"I told you once."

Bourke smiled as he lay there, saying presently, "You were wrong about it being Little Red Riding Hood. The wolf ate her."

"Did he?"

Bourke closed his eyes, no longer trying to worry out the riddle of his arrest. He simply wasn't letting himself think about it, for he didn't like the way his thoughts always reverted to a nagging suspicion of either Cass, Kate Banks or Eleanor having talked about him too freely. All three knew how important it had been to him to keep his identity hidden and he wasn't letting himself lose faith in any one of them.

Instead of trying to see what deception lay behind him he was looking ahead, planning on how he would deal with Drury. Sometime tonight sleep would crowd the deputy out of his vigilance. When that happened Bourke was going to leave the stage. All he needed was two seconds. In those two seconds he would sit up, lift his boots and kick Drury in the face; not too hard, only hard enough to smash his head back against the panelling and knock him out. He had already gingerly tested the seat brace and knew it wouldn't take much strength to tear it loose and free himself.

The swaying of the coach against its thorough-braces slackened now and he heard the teams slowing to a walk, the sound of their hooves muffled by the steady drone of the rain. The road was evidently winding up another mountain shoulder along some deep canyon, for they made several turns not many minutes apart.

Bourke was watching Red Drury reaching to a pocket of his coat for tobacco when the lamp-glow was suddenly blocked out by a shadow to leave the inside of the coach dark.

The blast came without warning that instant—a bright flash of powder-flame stabbing in at the window, an ear-splitting concussion, a splintering of wood all blended in one sudden riot of sound.

Red Drury's throaty scream welled across out of the blackness, the driver yelled stridently. Bourke was straightening when the shotgun exploded a second time.

Now the shadow blocking out the lamp-glow moved away. Bourke briefly glimpsed the seat opposite torn to shreds of leather and horsehair stuffing. A red stain marked the spot where Drury had sat and there was a hole all the way through the hickory bracing on the side from which Bourke had moved. The deputy's shape, indistinct in the faint light, lay sprawled along the seat.

On the heel of that second shot Bourke heard something thud against the roof. The coach gave a vicious lurch as the teams bolted hard aside to the road's edge.

All at once the Concord tilted, the ground dropped from beneath its wheels and it went over, falling into a pit of blackness.

Five

THE CONCORD took the force of that sheer ten-foot drop squarely on its side. A rear wheel buckled, the back boot brace snapped, a corner of the top collapsed and the coach went on over with a pair of horses down for good and the remaining two thrashing to a stand.

Bourke was half-lying on the inside of the roof, his weight hanging by the handcuffs, when the vehicle began its second cartwheel. The doubletree snapped suddenly with a report like a gunshot, the Concord's flailing tongue bowling over one lunging animal and hurling him to his death on the rocks far below.

That second fall was shorter but more vicious than the first. Afterward, its momentum carried the coach end over end for three complete turns. There was a sudden smashing jolt as it rolled hard against something solid and immovable. Its right panels and door were stove in and Bourke crashed chest-down against a tangle of splintered wood and small granite shards. The wreck tipped, settled back again. A top-stay snapped and its jagged end raked the length of Bourke's right arm with a pain like the swipe of a hot branding iron.

Then an awesome stillness settled down, heightened by the steady murmur of the rain.

Bourke rolled slowly to his knees, the wind driven out of him and his chest aching as he gagged for a breath. He felt a dampness along his right sleeve and gingerly moved that arm, chuckling crazily when he found the handcuffs dangling from his wrist. That sound of his own voice brought back his sanity; and at once he was telling himself, *Stay where you are!*

He settled back again, shoulders against the sprung panelling of the coach's front wall now as he listened. From above he caught the sudden ring of an iron-shod hoof against rock and, when it didn't come again, decided that one of the horses must still be alive and trapped on that upper ledge.

But he was waiting for another sound and presently it came—the slow and rhythmic hoof-falls of a horse walking away down the road. For better than two minutes his hearing clung to that fading cadence; and when distance finally muted it completely he was almost sure that the killer had gone on.

Still, he was taking no chances. He stayed as he was, listening warily, knowing that his keeping utterly quiet might mean the difference between living or dying, knowing too that he was supposed to be dead. His arm gradually lost its numbness and, feeling of it again, he found the thick muscle along the forearm badly gashed and bleeding.

It was while he was moving around, leaning over to pull the bandana from his hip pocket, that one of his boots touched something soft and yielding, Red Drury's body. He didn't like what he had to do but forced himself to it. First he fumbled for the key in the deputy's vest and took off the handcuffs. Then came something else. Strangely enough, Red's .45 Colt's was still snugly rammed in holster. Bourke pulled the shell-belt from the dead man's waist and buckled it about his own. Now he felt a little better, less helpless.

During the next quarter hour the rain lessened, finally stopped. After that tedious interval had passed without his hearing any stray sound, he came stiffly erect and with his shoulder carefully and quietly forced open the coach's sky-facing door. Even more carefully he climbed out, his boots settling to the uncertain footing of a slide of rock and rubble. He wanted to light a match but didn't dare; and in the end he reached down into the coach, found his folded poncho and pulled it on. Wrapping it close around him against the bite of the damp air, he sat with his back against the Concord's muddy underside.

He had no way of knowing where he was—how far below the road, how close to another drop-off, which way he dared walk or crawl. Abruptly a sound shuttling down from above turned him rigid. Then he let out a long relieved breath as he finally realized that what he had heard was the horse moving around up there somewhere again. And now his loneliness didn't weigh so heavily. Some other living thing had come through those awful seconds alive; it didn't matter that it was an animal. He hoped the horse wasn't badly hurt.

That started him thinking of the driver, wondering if he still lived. He remembered that sound of something bumping against the stage's roof there directly after the second shot and, not wanting to believe it, his conviction was that the driver had been killed. He had the feeling he should be doing something about making sure of this; but he couldn't move from here through the pitch black night.

As the minutes ran slowly by, his tension eased and he was suddenly so tired he couldn't keep his eyes open. He dozed and once came wide awake thinking he had heard from a great distance the pound of a gunshot. He decided the sound had come out of a dream and now he lay more comfortably on his side, back to the belly of the Concord, and fell at once into a deep and dreamless sleep.

Again it was a sound that wakened him, his nerves tight with an undefined expectancy. He sat up and reached in under the poncho for the Colt's, quietly examining it and making sure that it was loaded. Then he sat there not knowing what he was expecting might happen.

Now he noticed that a faint greyness thinned the cobalt of the star-dusted sky over the mountainside rising steeply before him and realized he must have been asleep for several hours. The cold had stiffened the poncho and where it touched his neck it was like ice against his skin. He stood up finally and stretched and swung his arms to take the chill from his long frame. His right arm was stiff and throbbing dully. Moving it made it feel better. Once he caught a whisper of sound from close above. The horse up there was still alive.

Gradually the pitch blackness about him took on a greyish tinge and with the strengthening false dawn he began to make out the shapes of rock and earth across a slowly broadening radius from the coach.

The first important thing he saw was the driver's body. It was wedged between two boulders half buried by a talus-slide ten feet above him and obliquely to the right. The broken slump of the body told him the man was dead. Presently, looking some thirty feet above, he could make out the horse's head and shoulders showing over the line of the ledge that was edged with shoots of new grass. Close above the ledge showed the straight rim of the road against a dark backdrop of pines.

Now he could see the outcrop that had saved him, the upthrust shoulder of granite against which the Concord had slid down this loose talus to become wedged. Far downward, straight down almost, the tops of pines were showing through the grey light that filtered into a deep canyon. The awesomeness of that drop was too much to contemplate and he turned his glance away.

He could see a way up onto the ledge now and, carefully picking his footing, he started up there. Halfway up across the loose rubble he stopped briefly and shed the poncho.

Once he gained the ledge a savage fury briefly held him at sight of the pair of dead horses lying there. They were already stiff-legged. One had a broken neck, the other had been kicked to death by his harness-mate. There was no sign of the third horse. But the fourth, a sorrel gelding, was sound and unhurt, standing with broken reins trailing from his bit. And there was an easy way up off the foot of the ledge across the talus-slide to the road.

On the road presently, the gelding beside him, Bourke took one last wondering look into the canyon. He hardly believed even now, probably no one else would ever believe, that a man had walked away from the Concord's shattered hulk. He thought about Red and the driver, about going down there and burying them beneath the rubble. But for a definite reason he wanted someone to find them there, wanted their bodies in plain sight as mute evidence that he, like they, had died in the wreck of the stage. If anyone was interested enough, a party might be sent up here to dig through the rubble and search the deep bed of the canyon on the theory that his body had been thrown clear. Meantime, he was a dead man to everyone but Cass and Eleanor—and possibly Kate Banks; he hadn't made up his mind about Kate yet.

It was a fairly simple task for him to find the killer's tracks. The rain had washed out some of the sign; but where the man had put his horse behind a cedar-clump close above the road to wait for the stage the markings were plain, even to boot-prints and the stub of a cigarette.

The tracks the killer had made riding away were

plainer still. The man had gambled on the rain lasting. It hadn't. So Bourke presently slanted down out of the trees deciding he would rather know where the man had gone from here than learn where he had come from.

Sunlight was capping the timbered hill on the canyon's far shoulder before Bourke's slow pace had carried him a quarter mile. He was hungry and cold and so constantly aware of the complaint of his arm that finally he put his hand inside his shirt, letting his belt carry the arm's weight. That relieved the pain somewhat. Then he thought of the .45, of how useless it would be as it was now, worn at his right side; for the fingers of that hand were stiff. So he took the weapon from holster and thrust it through his belt under the right arm, knowing he must sight and fire it left-handed if at all. After thumbing half a dozen shells from the loops of Drury's belt, he tossed belt and empty holster into a thicket of scrub oak beside the road.

He couldn't stop shivering until the road made a turning that put him on a hill's eastward slope and in a blaze of sunlight. He stopped the horse there, soaking in the warmth, relishing it as he would have relished a meal. Looking downward he could see the road twisting its way through the lower foothills.

When he rode on it was with a new-born impatience; and he kept the sorrel at a steady trot, stopping only now and then to scan the road and make sure the killer's tracks were there. It was at one such halt that he found the sign gone.

Puzzled, he turned and rode slowly back. There were no tracks but those of the sorrel as he covered a hundred yards, another. Then he came to a cross-wash and found that he had ridden straight past a maze of confusing sign.

First, the shoe-prints of a new animal slanted out of the wash where a run of water had last night crossed the road, filling in the ruts and pouring over the road's edge downward across a gentle twenty-foot slope to the bed of the shallow hill fold below. Next, Bourke saw that the hoof-prints he had been following swung sharply from the road at that point and straight down the slope. The way dirt and gravel had been sprayed behind the tracks told him that the animal had left the road at a lunging run. And here the sign of the second horse followed the line of the other.

He put the sorrel down off the road and along the slope. He came to a low-growing pinon that showed broken branches where the first horse had gone straight through it. Immediately beyond he pulled the sorrel in along the lip of a ten-foot-high bank. Part of the bank had fallen away. There was a scar of the cave-in up here at the edge and directly below a slanting mound of fresh black earth lying against the bank along the bottom of the depression.

He turned aside and found a place where the sorrel could slide down the bank, then rode back up to the point where the earth had fallen away. There was evidence that quite a volume of water had flowed down this shallow gully during the storm—branches and leaves were caught on exposed roots that crossed it—and at first Bourke decided that the bank had been undercut by the flood and thus caved in. But then when he noticed that very little of the earth at the foot of the mound had been washed away, which meant the bank had fallen in after the rain, he knew he'd been wrong. And now he picked up the two sets of tracks again along with the print of a wedge-heeled boot considerably larger than the one he had found there high above near the wrecked Concord.

There were things here he didn't understand. The enigma deepened a minute later when, riding a wide circle about the spot, he found only the one set of new hoof-prints going away down the wash. The others, the tracks he had followed on the road, had simply vanished.

He spent ten minutes looking for the point where that first set of tracks left this spot. He didn't find it. The rider had come straight to the edge of the bank above and the tracks of his horse were plentifully in evidence near the mound of earth in the depression. But the man hadn't ridden away from here, his horse hadn't walked away.

Suddenly, startlingly, Bourke had the answer. *He's still here!* The look in his deep brown eyes became grave and wondering as he once more looked toward that slanting mound of fresh earth.

The soberness was still written strongly on his lean face as he slid from the sorrel's back. He went to his knees and with his good hand began scooping aside the loose black dirt.

That early morning was like a hundred others to many people. Yet to a few it was one that would be long remembered.

A young prospector on his way out of Red Canyon, for instance, would in thirty years be telling his grandchildren how, at dawn that morning, he had carefully walked his horse in on a band of grazing antelope only to miss his meat because at the last moment the animals were spooked by a stray buffalo bull that unaccountably charged up out of a coulee and made for him.

And a bridge crew of the Sante Fe working in the Gorge would remember the day because, on arriving at work, they found their heavy tools gone. Later one of their big wooden chests was found wedged in the rocks below a rapids down-river and it was decided that Rio Grande men had climbed down into the Gorge during the night and taken this direct means of slowing their rival's work.

De Remer wouldn't soon forget the day, either. Sheriff Shaffer had returned to Canon by stage late last night, abruptly and unannounced. Acting on some obscure but reliable information, Shaffer had before breakfast this morning appeared at the express office to confiscate several cases of arms and ammunition intended for De Remer's guards up the main canyon. There was nothing De Remer could do about it.

When news of this reached the main Rio Grande camp up the canyon, there was talk of that night taking every man down to town to clear the streets and saloons of the last tough claiming allegiance to the Sante Fe. One of De Remer's guards at Spikebuck came up to Canyon Line's yard at mid-morning to discuss this possibility with Cass Ives. But Cass was only mildy interested in the railroad war; he was worried about Dan Exin, who this morning was out of his bunk and puttering about the blacksmith shanty with Jim Manlove; and he was very worried over Bourke's arrest.

A rider on his way up from the Spikebuck trail to Texas Creek brought the news of De Remer's bad luck to Kimbrell's tie camp shortly before ten. The crew was working the upper stacks along the river, sorting the burned and unburned ties, when the horseman came over from the road with his story. Shortly even the cook, wearing his flour-sacking apron, walked on up from the mess shack to see what all the fuss was about.

This left only one man in evidence at the shack. For the past several minutes he had been sitting on the doorstep, a rifle leaning against the wall at his elbow. Now as the cook walked up the road this man picked up the rifle and sauntered to the shack's corner, looking off toward the others.

All this Bourke took in from a hundred yards downcanyon where he had been squatting at the foot of a shoulder-high outcropping of granite the past quarter hour. He had been led straight here by the sign of that second rider he had tracked down out of the hills and he had carefully circled the camp to discover that the hoofprints had gone no further along the road. So he had settled down to wait and watch the crew. Some ten minutes ago he had seen Ben Spohr, guarded by the man with the rifle, come from the shack and go out back to a stack of wood near the corral. Ben had carried several armloads of wood into the kitchen lean-to before going back into the shack again by way of the front door. The man with the rifle had put a padlock on the door. And Bourke knew then that for some unexplained reason Ben Spohr was being held a prisoner.

Spohr was the man he wanted to see, no one else. So now, with only the guard and Ben at the shack, he started walking in on it. The guard still stood there at the far corner, the shack's front was out of line with the rest of the crew, so all Bourke had to do was walk quietly and fast. Halfway in on the building he drew the Colt's from his belt.

He stopped at the down-river corner of the shack and

103

cocked the heavy .45. That sound brought the guard wheeling around.

The man froze, his eyes coming wide open. He had been caught flat-footed, the carbine's butt-plate grounded on the toe of his boot.

When Bourke said, "Come over here," he made no move for several seconds. Then, lifting the Winchester carefully from his boot, he came on toward the door as Bourke walked in on it from the other side.

Bourke stopped just short of the single broad step, drawling, "Better put it down."

The other bobbed his head and reached over to lean the rifle against the wall. "Now open up," Bourke said.

By the time the padlock was off and the door swinging open, Bourke was close behind the guard. He put the muzzle of the Colt's against the man's spine and pushed. They went in the door that way.

Ben Spohr sat at the far end of a big table that, with its benches, made up the furnishings of the barren room. Two face-up poker hands lay on the table in front of Spohr and as he saw Bourke his big hands went motionless in surprise. Then, deliberately, he laid the cards aside and folded his hands, smiling thinly at the guard and drawling, "Got a way with him, hasn't he, Phil?"

The guard made no answer as Bourke closed the door and leaned back against it. "Spohr," Bourke said, "where did you spend the night?"

A mask of impassiveness at once settled across Spohr's blocky features. "So he tried it, did he?" came his enigmatic words, so low-spoken Bourke barely caught them.

Bourke said. "Talk. What about last night?"

Once again a smile broke across Spohr's face. He looked at Bourke over the space of several seconds before his answer came. "I wasn't where you think." His glance shifted to the guard. "Phil, tell him where I was."

Phil's eyes hadn't strayed from the weapon now hanging at Bourke's side. "Right here," he said in a hollow voice.

Bourke took that in, at length asking, "Why?"

Spohr's heavy shoulders lifted, fell. "Tell him, Phil."

The guard's glance rose to meet Bourke's now. "Boss's orders. None of us could figure it out."

"He was here the whole night?" Bourke insisted.

Phil nodded. "Since eight, when Smitty brought the word out."

"What word?"

"That we was to de-horn Ben and hold him here."

Once more Bourke's glance moved around to Spohr. "Why?" he asked again.

Spohr smiled crookedly. "I wouldn't do a certain job for Tom. He's got something on me, same as he has on most of us. So he's turning me over to the law."

Bourke was feeling a rebirth of the respect this man had stirred in him the night of the fire here. He saw how careful Spohr had been in answering his questions just now, making sure that the answers weren't his and open to doubt. He had unquestionably been here last night and not along the road in the Greenhorns as Bourke had halfway suspected.

"So you weren't up in the hills," Bourke drawled. "Who was?"

"How would I know?"

"There was a man with you that first night you jumped me. Who was he?"

"Bates."

"He's dead now," Bourke said flatly. "Around midnight he shot up a stage I was riding in. The driver was killed. So was Red Drury, the sheriff's right bower. So was I supposed to be."

"No!" Strong surprise and a strange visible anger held Spohr wordless for several moments. Then: "Red was too good a man to die that way. Bates cashed in, too?"

"He did. Not then but later. This morning I backtracked him. Someone had waited for him below along the road. He had the top of his head blown off. He and his horse are buried up there under a caved-in cutbank." Bourke paused long enough to let that sink in. Then: "Who killed him, Ben?"

Spohr was no longer showing any surprise. "You guess," he drawled.

"I followed the killer's sign straight back here. Who showed up here early this morning?"

Once again Spohr looked across at Kimbrell's crewman. This time he only nodded; and without further prompting Phil said, "No one but the boss, was there?"

"Kimbrell?" The paralysis of strong surprise held Bourke wordless a moment. "Where is he now?"

"Gone," Spohr said. "Back to town probably."

"He changed horses?"

Ben nodded. "And ate a big breakfast."

Bourke was baffled, uncertain of himself now, hardly believing what they had told him. "But why?" he asked angrily. "Why Kimbrell? Sure, I helped put the match to this layout that night. All right, he'd asked for that. Would he cut me down for that slim a reason?"

"Friend, if I knew how Tom's think tank worked, I wouldn't be in the spot I'm in now." . . . Spohr was serious . . . "Sometimes he's that way, *loco* as they come. Don't ask me why."

Bourke's thinking was becoming muddled. Abruptly he noticed that the gun was still in his hand. He lifted it and thrust it in his belt. "That's all you can give me?"

"Hell, it's enough, isn't it? All you've got to do is walk up on him, get close enough so you can't miss. Or let the sheriff handle it."

"There's more to it than that," Bourke said wearily. He eased out from the door now and opened it. "There's a rifle out here, Ben. I'm taking it with me. Give me two minutes to get set and I'll cover you while you make a run for it."

An awed look touched Spohr's eyes. "This is a four ace hand for me, Rold," he said quietly. "How come?"

"I pay back my debts."

"The other night, you mean?" Spohr shook his head. "You had nothin' to do with that. Or next to nothing."

Bourke made little sense of this but only watched as Spohr's glance dropped to the cards lying on the table. When the man's eyes lifted again there was a bleak look in them. "Once I killed a man," he said quietly. "That's what Tom's got on me. You don't easy forget a thing like that. It keeps comin' back to you at the damnedest times. Like the other night. I couldn't pull those triggers. Maybe I was thinking how you hadn't beat my face in when you had the chance. But it was this other mostly."

He paused briefly, then went on, "Tom's different. A thing like that wouldn't bother him. Nothing does."

Bourke had a thought then that made him say, "Selling out the Rio Grande on his last contract didn't bother him."

"No. That's what I'm saying. Nothing does."

"Will he sell out again?"

Spohr lifted his hands from the table, let them fall. "Who knows? He's trying to. This time Watrous isn't so free with his change. They're still talkin' terms." He gave Bourke a measuring glance. "But I'm trying to tell you something else about him. Don't give him a chance. Go straight on in and find him and get your chore over with. Even if you have to shoot him in the back. He made a try for you last night. If you don't get him first, he'll get you."

"But why would he want to?"

"Search me. What's he had against some others I know? Ames, for instance. Or—"

"Frank Ames?" Bourke cut in, his eyes gone flinty. "What about him?"

Ben shrugged. "Maybe nothing. That's it, you never know with Tom. He's careful. But I was with him the night Ames turned up missing. We'd met Ames up the road here, eight or ten miles above. He was on his way back to the yard, drivin' a wagon. He and Tom started talking over that deal Tom's been after, buying the outfit. I got tired listening and drifted on ahead."

When he hesitated, Bourke said tonelessly, "Go on." That excitement of a moment ago had died and now he felt dead inside, almost dreading what was to come.

Spohr shook his head now. "That's all I know for sure. Except that Tom never caught up with me on the way back to town that night. And I was goin' along slow, waiting for him. The next day they fished Ames out of the river."

It was habit with Kate that made her take the side path

down the yard that early evening and enter the house by way of the office. She was closing the door of the darkening room, a basketful of groceries over her other arm, when Bourke came up out of the rocker that stood with its back to her.

"Hello, Kate," he said.

She swung around, startled, breathing involuntarily, gladly, "Oh, Bourke!" She showed him that strong unguarded emotion before a definite reserve settled through her. Then she was saying lifelessly, "So you did get away."

That queer change in her had its immediate effect on him. He thought he knew what she was thinking and would have liked to say something to strike out the thought. But her strange coolness put a halter on his urge. So he only lifted his arm, showing her the torn dark-stained sleeve, drawling, "Yes, I got away. With this."

Her glance no longer met his as she set the basket aside and crossed the shadowed room to a big glass-fronted cabinet lined with shelves of instruments and medicines. As she opened the cabinet's door she said matter-of-factly, "Take off your coat."

He hung the coat from the back of the chair and, coming across to her, rolled his shirt-sleeve high along his arm. She turned to a sink beyond the cabinet and pumped a basin full of water. "Over here," she said.

His soberness was matching hers as he went to stand beside her. She soaped a clean rag and taking his wrist, began washing the dried blood from the swollen gash on his forearm. The light was bad, for dusk was well on the way. Still, she could see well enough to say presently, "This is badly infected. How did you get it?"

"Caught it on a piece of wood."

He could tell by the added weight of her touch against his arm that his vague answer irritated her. At length she dried the arm with a fresh towel. Then she took a bottle from the cabinet, staining a piece of folded gauze with some dark liquid from it. "This is going to hurt," she warned him. And she quickly swabbed the gash along its whole length.

He knotted his fist and stiffened the arm, catching his breath sharply as the pain struck all the way to his shoulder. She looked up at once, an apology and a momentary tenderness in her eyes. "I'm sorry, Bourke. That wasn't necessary." Then suddenly she threw the gauze into the sink, bursting out, "Why don't you say something?"

"What is there to say?"

"Anything! Don't just stand there letting me wonder."

"Wonder, Kate? What are you wondering?"

"If you really are a deserter! Why you're here instead of at the sheriff's office!" She gave him a pleading look. "They've just brought the bodies back, Bourke. They're up there trying to find yours. There's some ugly talk about you. Red Drury and Bart Hansen were well liked."

He considered that a moment. "This talk. Is it that I killed them and made a getaway?"

"They say it's possible." She stood for a moment looking at him. Then she pointed to the table alongside the door. "Why do you suppose I'm working on you here in the dark instead of lighting that lamp?"

"I wondered."

"Because I don't want anyone to see you here. I'm afraid for you, Bourke."

"Thank you," he drawled, meaning it. "Maybe it's best no one does see me. But not for the reason you think."

"Then why?"

He studied her shadowed face, reading the deep concern so plainly written on it as he asked soberly, "Kate, how much does Tom Kimbrell mean to you?"

Puzzlement eased her worried expression. "He's a good friend, nothing more. Why should you ask?"

"The other night you said he'd asked you to marry him."

She nodded and a faint worried smile drew out the pleasing line of her lips. "I was angry at what you'd said. But I'm not marrying him, if that's what you're trying to get me to say."

"You're sure of that?"

"Very. But does it matter to you?"

Instead of answering he reached across with his left hand and clumsily fumbled in the pocket of his coat for his pipe. Quite suddenly he was longing for the taste of tobacco and it was with some surprise that he realized he hadn't had a smoke the whole day—not since up there in the hills last night in the stage before the wreck. Today he had been so continually on edge, so tense, that he hadn't once thought of the pipe.

He drew it out now, his touch telling him something was wrong with it even before he looked down to see that it was broken, the stem at an odd angle to the split shank of the briar.

Kate looked at it. "Why, it's broken."

"Just one more thing," he drawled ruefully, knowing it must have been broken in the wreck. He added the obscure comment, "Part of the reason I'm glad your mind isn't set on Kimbrell."

"What does a pipe have to do with what I think of Tom?" she asked impatiently. "Bourke, will you please tell me what you're going to without making me wait!"

He nodded. "I had to be sure." He breathed a long slow sigh now, hating what was coming yet knowing it was inevitable.

"Kate, maybe you can help me straighten out something," he began. "About Kimbrell. Yesterday he found out from someone, I don't know who, about my resigning that commission. Remember our talking about it the other night?"

Her hurt and puzzled look erased the small doubt in him even before she said, "He didn't find out from me, Bourke. You said you didn't want anyone to know about you."

"I know," Bourke said quickly. "But someone did tell him. My resignation hasn't gone through yet, as I told you. I have no papers. Now he and I don't agree on certain things. Chiefly in a business way," was how he put it. "He saw a way of framing this desertion charge on me, of getting me out of the way. So he—"

"How can you be sure of what you're saying," Kate cut in hotly, "sure it was Tom?" As she spoke she crossed the room and sat in the rocker by the window, her glance not leaving him.

"Never mind," he told her, "I am sure. That's neither

here nor there. But it does tie in with what happened last night."

He drew in a deep breath. "We were on a stretch of road hanging along one of those deep cuts. The driver may have been asleep for all I know. It was late, almost midnight. All of a sudden someone rode alongside and fired a load of buckshot through the window. It got Red, killed him instantly. It would have caught me, too, if I hadn't changed to the other seat a while back. This man killed the driver next. With a shotgun, Kate! You know what that does to a man."

Her eyes were wide with alarm now as he went on, "The horses bolted and we left the road, fell partway into this canyon. The coach wouldn't do for matchwood now. For a reason I'll never know, all I got out of it was this." He lifted his arm.

She was wordless a long moment before asking in a hushed voice, "Who could have done it?"

"A man by the name of Bates," he told her. "This morning I followed his sign back down the road. Someone had been waiting for him below. He'd been shot, along with his horse. Buried off the road in a place no one would ever look for him."

"How awful!" she breathed. "Then there was another man with him?"

"There was. But Bates didn't know it. He was killed so he'd never talk."

"And the other man? Who was he?"

"I'll get to that. When I was sure what had happened to the first, to Bates, I started following the second. He led me straight to Kimbrell's tie-camp up there this side of Texas Creek. You know it?"

She nodded mutely and in the faint light he thought he saw her oval face losing color. He was suddenly impatient to have this over with.

"Here it is, Kate, all of it. I'd been thinking of one man who might have done it. He bore me a grudge, a real grudge. He seemed the likeliest bet, in fact the only one. But when I went in there it was to find that this man had been locked up under guard since early last night. He and

Kimbrell had a falling out and Kimbrell was holding him for the sheriff."

"Who was he?"

"Ben Spohr."

"I know him," she said at once. "He's evil looking, the kind you would—"

"Forget his looks," he said impatiently. "Anyway, Spohr couldn't have done it. There was only one man who could. He rode in there early this morning. No one else had arrived there since last night. He was the only one, Kate. It's important to remember that."

He paused now, groping for a gentle way of saying what had to be said. The office was so still that he could hear the steady ticking of the clock from one of the other rooms. And into this stillness Kate spoke with a small voice:

"Bourke, are you trying to tell me it was Tom?"

He sighed and nodded. He stood there wordless, loathing himself for not moving his glance from her ashen face.

"You really believe it, don't you?" came her muted words after a brief silence.

"I didn't want to. But I had to."

Again, the silence settled down oppressively. She was no longer looking at him but at her slender hands folded in her lap. Then she said quietly, "Bourke, I've had a horrible day. It was because of you. My first patient this morning could talk of nothing but your arrest. He was a friend of Red Drury's. Of course he didn't know then about Red. I—I simply couldn't believe what he told me, that you were a deserter."

She paused a moment, her glance still directed downward. Then she went on in that same low but intent way, "I had to know the truth. You see, Bourke, it mattered to me. I remembered your fiancee, even remembered her name. So, like a little fool, I walked up to the hotel and saw her. She was—well, distant to begin with. And quite curious over my knowing you. I think she enjoyed telling me what she did."

When she said nothing more, Bourke asked, "What was that?"

Slowly her glance lifted to him. He was dumbfounded to see her eyes brimming with tears. "She said that you really were a deserter, Bourke. She said she hadn't known it when she came here to meet you."

He was shocked. Yet he managed to ask, "And you believed her?"

"What else was there for me to believe?" Her voice was brittle and her expression had hardened out of its gentleness. "Now you tell me that a man I like very much is a killer! He can't be, Bourke! Do you understand? He can't!"

All at once he realized the futility of trying to convince her. "All right Kate," he said wearily.

His words did nothing to ease her anger and now her hands gripped the chair arms as she breathed, "I've been a fool! Just an infatuated, blind, love-struck fool! Letting myself like a tall stranger who stands straight and seems gentle and kind and acts the way I've always thought a man should act! Oh, I can say these things now! Tell you how I've looked up to you because of what you did for Cass Ives. And because of why you're here. I was happy with you the other night, Bourke. As happy as I've ever been!"

Her rising voice broke suddenly. When she went on it was lower-pitched, edged with a scorn that was almost loathing. "Now you take the word of a worthless person like Spohr that Tom Kimbrell has murdered three men in cold blood. Did—"

"Not three, Kate. Only Bates." Bourke paused, then added quietly, "And Frank."

"Frank? Your brother?"

He nodded, saying nothing.

She stared at him incredulously an instant. Then all at once she burst out laughing. There was hysteria in her voice, it quickly became high-pitched, uncontrollable, and when her laughing kept on Bourke stepped quickly over to her chair and took her by the shoulders, roughly shaking her. "Stop that, Kate!"

She began sobbing then, brokenly and with her head lowered. "Get out, Bourke!" she managed to say. "Let me alone. Please! I mean it. Get out! And I hope they catch you." Her head came up to let him see her tear-filled eyes blazing with hate. "Do you hear? I hope you're caught! They'll—"

She stiffened as a sound of slurring steps shuttled in from the gravelled walk beyond the door. Bourke was slowly turning in that direction when someone knocked.

Kate gave him a bitter, triumphant look as she rose from the chair. She wiped her eyes. She went to the door, opened it wide. The light out there was strong enough to show Bourke a slat-bodied man of middle age who quickly reached up to take off his wide-brimmed hat as Kate was saying, "Good evening. Won't you come in?"

"Can't do it, Kate," he said. "I'm in a hurry. Been in a hurry all day or I'd of got around to see you sooner." He paused momentarily, then blurted out, "This is the damnedest thing that's happened around Canon in a long time, Kate. I can't get over it. We'll all miss him like a brother. It should've been someone else—me, anyone but Mark. I'm sorrier'n I can say."

"That's the nicest thing anyone's said of Dad," Kate told him.

The man was obviously not at his ease. He fingered his hat-brim and now the nervous movement of his hands brushed his coat open slightly.

Bourke saw the nickelled star pinned to the vest underneath the coat.

Then Kate was saying, "Won't you come in a moment, Sheriff?"

Six

As she spoke, Kate stepped back from the door. And there settled through Bourke a feeling of such utter helplessness, of such complete weariness, that nothing seemed to matter.

Then Sheriff Shaffer was saying, "Kate, I'd like to. But there's so much doin' I can't spare even a minute. You heard about Red?"

She nodded.

"Queerest thing I ever run onto," the law man went on. "We've been over that gulch with a fine-tooth comb. If this man's there, his body is hung in the top of a tree. I've sent up to Silver Cliff to get old Al Rush down to help us. Don't like the looks of it. Not a-tall."

"You think he got away?"

"What I think don't matter much, Kate. But if he did—" He let a moment's silence eloquently take the place of words. "Well, I'll be moseyin' along. Girl, if there's the least thing I can do, let me know."

"I will, Ben."

She stood looking along the path as he walked away. Finally she turned. She was looking at Bourke as she slowly closed the door and then leaned back against it as though too weak to stand without support. "Now you know what I think of you," she murmured.

"I know."

"He could have come in and arrested you. I'd have let him."

"Then why didn't you tell him I was in here?"

The measuring look her green eyes had fixed on him altered perceptibly. "That would have been different, wouldn't it? Like a little girl tattling. Can you understand that?"

"Maybe I can." He was rolling the sleeve of his shirt down over his bare arm.

"You'll need a bandage for that," she said quietly. "Let me fix it."

"It'll do as it is." He buttoned the sleeve and reached for his coat.

She watched him shrug it onto his broad shoulders. Then all at once she was saying, "I want more than I've ever wanted anything to believe in you, Bourke. But you're asking too much of me."

He looked across at her soberly. There was nothing to say.

"Where will you go now?" she asked.

"To find Kimbrell. After that—" He shrugged.

She looked straight at him, her glance oddly probing. "There may be no 'after that,' Bourke. I suppose I should do something to stop it. But a woman has no right interfering in a thing like this, has she?"

Her words were more a statement than a question and seemed to need no answer. Bourke took his hat from the windowsill and turned toward her again. She opened the door and stepped aside.

He came on past her with a sudden and strong physical awareness of her. She stood tall and straight, quite beautiful and infinitely desirable; but what she had said, what she believed of him, gave her a remoteness now that held her far beyond his reach.

He knew she had spoken her last word. Halfway down the path he crowded back the impulse to turn and go back and make one last try at convincing her. Yet he saw how twisted were the facts—she already had Kimbrell's and Eleanor's word, and now the sheriff's, against his. Regardless of what she had thought or wanted to think of him, she couldn't overlook the word of at least two people she had known and trusted for so long.

He turned along the street with the shadows of dusk deepening about him, more clearly than anything else remembering her straightforward admission of what her feelings toward him had been until today. And now he realized that never between him and Eleanor had there been a depth of emotion comparable to this. Perhaps it was because the path of their courtship had been so smooth —until now.

For the first time he was thinking of what Eleanor had said of him today as something quite apart from its effect on Kate. And there built up in him a steadily rising resentment and anger, along with a bafflement that left him far short of understanding her motives. This afternoon he had stopped at Canyon Line's yard to see Cass. Unfortunately Cass hadn't been in, but his instinct told him Cass would never have betrayed the trust he put in him in giving the information leading to his arrest. And only minutes ago Kate had proven that she hadn't betrayed her trust in him. That left only Eleanor.

Here was something so important to him, its implications so unsettling, that seeing her suddenly became even more important than finding Kimbrell, more important than anything.

He turned up the cross-street to Main and, once there, chose the side with the most darkened windows to walk along. He realized how noticeable his torn coat-sleeve must be and put his right hand in the pocket of his trousers. When he came to the narrow stairway entrance leading up to the lobby of the *McClure House* he went on past to the corner, taking the side-street and continuing on back. There, in the deep shadow, he paused a moment at the walk's edge to look up to Eleanor's corner sitting room. A narrow wrought-iron balcony ran the length of the building's front and side, and through the grillework he saw the drawn shade of her window aglow with lamplight.

There was no one in the hotel's kitchen-entrance or the narrow hallway beyond as he stepped in out of the alley. He was halfway up the darkened stairway to the lobby floor when someone crossed the hallway below, calling, "That you, Bob?" He didn't answer and in another moment turned out of the head of the stairway along the dimly lit corridor above.

Eleanor's door stood well ajar and strong lamplight shone across the hallway's ornate carpeting. Bourke lightly tapped the open panel, and from the adjoining bedroom Eleanor's voice answered, "It's open."

He came on into the room and as an afterthought turned to shut the door. More plainly now, Eleanor, said, "Just bring the boxes on in here and—"

He faced about to see her coming to an abrupt halt in the entrance to the bedroom. Her astonishment when she saw who it was turned her face a chalky white. She wore a dark blue velveteen dress, severely plain, its long sleeves carelessly rolled above her elbows and its high collar unbuttoned so low that the creamy whiteness of her neck was exposed to the shadowed hollow between her breasts.

She caught her breath and now with one hand pulled the neck of the dress together as her other brushed back from her forehead a tawny wisp that had escaped the carelessly gathered knot of hair at the back of her head. Bourke had never seen her at an unguarded moment like this, her untidiness all the more striking because he had always thought of her as being perfectly groomed.

"I can come back later if you'd rather," he said.

"No. No, Bourke." Her words were spoken quickly and in confusion. She made a visible effort to regain her composure then, nodding to the settee along the near wall. "Won't you sit down?"

"Doesn't matter."

He didn't move; and now she felt the weight of his steady glance and a tide of color rushed back into her face. "I . . . I was about to begin dressing for dinner," she said lamely.

His brows lifted in a polite query. "Really? And what about the boxes?" He was looking beyond her into the bedroom, seeing the big open trunk that stood before the dresser, its packed top tray bulging. And just then Gretchen moved briefly into sight, giving him a startled glance and drawing quickly back again.

"I was out shopping this afternoon," she said. "They were to send some things here to the room."

The barest trace of a smile touched his dark eyes and he drawled, "How much time have you before the train leaves, Eleanor? Or is it a stage? You should travel by stage more often. It can be quite exciting."

She couldn't overlook this double meaning. And now her head lifted in a proud tilt and she said evenly, "I suppose I had that coming. Yes, if you must know it, I'm taking the night train. It leaves at nine."

He nodded. "Then get on with your packing."

She reached behind her and drew shut the bedroom door, saying with some dignity, "Gretchen can finish it." She was calmer now, drawing on the reserve of her assurance and good manners as she murmured, "We do have some things to talk over, don't we?"

"Yes." He said no more than that, waiting for her to continue.

She leaned back against the wall now, unconsciously striking a graceful pose. Perhaps it was also unconsciously that she lowered the hand that held the dress together. Dishevelled as she was, she made a picture that would have taken any man's eye.

She said quietly, "I've been terribly worried, Bourke. They said you might have died. Now I'm sorry I let this happen. At the time I thought I was doing the right thing."

"Then you know what did happen?"

She nodded gravely, in humility almost, her glance not flinching. "If you'd like I'll tell them it was all a lie."

"You knew what Kimbrell was doing?"

"Yes. We planned it together." Her voice lost its meek quality as she added, "It would have come out all right in the end if only you'd not broken away. Dad would have smoothed over everything."

"So you believe it, too?" he softly drawled.

"Believe what?"

"That I killed those men."

"Didn't you?"

He smiled, shaking his head. "It doesn't matter now, Eleanor. It's finished. There's only one more thing. Why didn't you tell Kate Banks the truth above me?"

Her eyes came brightly alive. "She would have told everyone! Besides, she was meddling."

"It so happens that I want her to know the truth."

For an instant she appeared startled. Then her blue eyes took on a chill, disdainful look. "What does she mean to you, Bourke?"

"Not what you're thinking," he stated flatly, a strange anger in him. "But if she ever does think of me again I want it to be without this."

Her glance narrowed shrewdly. "I couldn't believe it then. But now I do," she said softly. "I had the impression she was about to burst into tears."

He said nothing; and she read into his silence a definite meaning. For she went on in that precise, cool way she had when she was pressing an advantage, "We're engaged, Bourke. Have you forgotten?"

"No, I've not forgotten."

"If you haven't, how does it happen that a girl has become so ... so interested in you that she can act that way?"

"That's enough, Eleanor."

"You'll listen whether you like it or not!" she flared, her eyes blazing an outright defiance now. "Never have I been so humiliated! To have that woman brazenly tell me I was lying when—"

She hadn't caught herself in time. And now Bourke asked quietly, "When you accused me of desertion, Eleanor?"

She was on her guard again and with a sudden restless impatience walked out across the room, saying, "Must you pick at me? No, of course I didn't mean that." She wheeled abruptly toward him, her full skirt billowing, then swirling tight around her to show him the fullness and perfection of her figure. "Bourke, we must stop this bickering! It's killing something between us!"

"I'm afraid it is."

She came over to him, her hands clenching his arms so that he winced at the stab of pain along his bad shoulder. "Come with me tonight, Bourke! Get away from this dreadful place. You can get on the train as it's pulling out of the station. No one here knows you. By tomorrow this will all be behind us and we can begin forgetting."

He was feeling the strong pull of her hold on him, of memories that were altogether pleasant and still exciting. But then as he looked down at her, seeing her against the background of the last two days, he suddenly and with a terrible certainty realized that everything had changed between them.

He said, as gently as he could, "No, Eleanor. I'm not going with you."

"You're staying here?" she asked incredulously. "You still think you can do something about Frank?"

"It's already done."

"Then what's to keep you?"

He lifted his hands outward in a spare gesture of finality. "I couldn't begin to answer that. All I know is that I belong here."

"But they think you're a killer!"

"They'll forget that." He couldn't help but add, "After you tell them the truth."

All at once, as she stood there still unbelieving and aghast, it seemed intolerable to him to prolong the absurdity of this moment, to add to its awkwardness. He said, "Goodbye," and stepped around her toward the door.

She called in a hushed exclamation, "Bourke!" He halted and looked around.

"Bourke, if you do this to me you can never come back!"

"No, I suppose not."

"I mean it, Bourke! Never!"

He tilted his head in a barely perceptible nod and, turning, went out of the room.

After Bourke had gone, Kate stood there by the office door for several minutes, the bewilderment and hurt so strong in her that she felt numb, completely worn out. Finally, when her thinking got her nowhere, she took the basket of groceries into the kitchen and lit the lamp there, hesitating as she tried to decide whether or not to bother eating at all.

Presently she went into the dining room and set a place at the table, hoping that a change from the meal-in-kitchen routine would improve both her appetite and her frame of mind. One of the patients today had brought her two dozen fresh eggs. She remembered a jar of green chili left over from last fall's canning and tried to relish the thought of an omelette.

But in the end she simply couldn't face the thought of food and wearily took the chair at the dining-table to sit staring blankly at the flowered design of the wallpaper across the room. Bourke's look as he had left the office kept coming back to her. The deep hurt and pride in him had showed so plainly that she couldn't forget it. And now, for the first time, in remembering it she was struck by doubts.

Thinking back on what he had told her she began to see a logic in it that had escaped her as they talked. She had been on the defensive then, with impressions gathered throughout the day too firmly rooted to be put so hastily aside. But she was putting them aside now—her regard for Tom Kimbrell, what Eleanor had said, the quick judgments of her friends after the tarp-covered wagon had delivered its grisly load at the undertaker's. Against all this she placed her instinctive liking for Bourke. And she had too much faith in herself, in her common sense, to ignore her feelings for him.

Gradually, logically, her viewpoint changed as she thought in this vein. At the very least she was uncertain now of the indictment she had built against him. And with this uncertainty placed alongside his claims she realized with a sudden, deep-striking regret how unfair her judgment of him might be. She could make out nothing through the fog of confused circumstance beyond that faintest possibility that she had done him a great wrong in doubting him along with his beliefs. Regardless of how mistaken he was, it was obvious that he believed what he had claimed of Kimbrell. It followed that these beliefs, although mistaken ones, needn't condemn Bourke. He had somehow been deceived. He was the same man as yesterday and the night before.

Once she realized how wrong she had been in condemning him, she became alarmed. She was at once remembering his quiet words as they parted. She thought fleetingly of Tom Kimbrell, not letting herself doubt him any more than she doubted Bourke, not letting herself believe him guilty of the things Bourke had mentioned. And suddenly she knew that she must do what she could to prevent any meeting between the two of them until the true facts were known.

She thought she knew where to look for Bourke and now she quickly rose from the table, took her coat from the walnut rack in the hall, and left the house. She started up the walk the long way of the block, intending to cut across the vacant corner lot toward Main Street and the hotel.

Tom Kimbrell, turning his buggy out of the side street below, saw her and in the fading light he recognized her slim figure and slapped the team to a smart trot.

The sound of the buggy touched only the surface of Kate's awareness and she didn't really notice it until it slanted in to the street's edge directly beyond her. Then Tom Kimbrell leaned out, saying, "Almost missed you, Kate. I was stopping by to call."

She noticed the typically gracious way he lifted his hat as he spoke and was thankful for the near-darkness that hid her look of outright relief as she walked over to the buggy. She was thinking of only one thing, of keeping him here, and it cost her a conscious effort to lie blithely now, "I was going for a walk, Tom."

"And I was calling around to see if you'd go for a drive," he told her.

"That would be nice." Her voice almost broke with the keenness of her relief. She found herself wondering how long Bourke would dare stay in town looking for Kimbrell when he knew he was being hunted. And, thinking of this, she said, "Let's get out into the country. I've felt so penned up all day."

"Good. We'll drive up along the rim." He stepped down now, still holding the reins, offering her a hand.

She gathered her skirts and let him help her onto the seat, the buggy tilting sharply against his weight as he swung up beside her. When he reached over to unfold the lap-robe on the seat between them she said quickly, "We won't need it, Tom. It isn't even cool yet."

He drawled, "Suit yourself," and took the whip from its socket, flicking it sharply so that the horses went from their stand to a trot at one stride. He was inordinately proud of this pair of matched blacks; they were pacers, he had brought them all the way from Kentucky, and now she was remembering how honestly thrilled she had been at their seemingly effortless speed that late afternoon last week when he had taken her for her first drive behind them down the Florence road.

"New moon up there," he said casually, keeping west along River Street toward the outskirts of town.

"With the evening star in her lap," Kate mused. She hadn't noticed the moon since night before last with Bourke when she had several times glimpsed it hanging over the far rim of the canyon before she went to sleep against his shoulder.

Presently, he asked, "Have you heard the news, Kate?"

"About Captain Rold? Yes."

He chuckled softly. "Wonder if he really was a captain? Well, he certainly had the wool pulled over our eyes."

She put down the abrupt impulse to ask him outright about the things Bourke had said of him this evening. But she couldn't help saying, "I wonder if he's dead."

"My bets would be the other way."

"Could he be the one who killed those men?"

"It's possible. But that's a strong thing to think of a man unless you know for sure."

It was a kind thing, a generous thing to say and Kate realized it with a real feeling of warmth toward him. And once more she had that urge to talk with him, to settle her doubts once and for all. A small warning voice cautioned her against it; but, over-wrought as she was, she didn't listen to it.

"Tom, I've seen Bourke Rold," she heard herself saying.

When his head came sharply around she knew it was too late to change her mind. "You've seen him? When?"

"Just now. Half an hour ago."

"Here in town?"

He tightened the reins and the team slowed to a walk. The houses on either side of the street were widely spaced now. Ahead, Kate could see the first stretch of open country, with the jagged line of the peaks still plain against the sky as she quietly said, "Don't stop, Tom. I want to talk with you."

Frowning and with a puzzled look he loosened the reins and the horses lifted slowly out of their walk again. He said nothing and without glancing his way she sensed his steady regard.

She carefully considered what she had to tell him and it was several moments before she spoke. "He said some terrible things about you, Tom," was how she put it finally. And now she looked around at him.

He smiled, a real humor in his eyes. "He would. The man has no cause to love me."

"I said terrible things, Tom."

"Just what?" He had sobered.

"First that this charge of desertion against him is untrue, that you were somehow behind it."

Surprisingly enough, he nodded at once. "I was. I wanted him out of here. He was getting too tangled up in my affairs." He gave her a reproachful glance. "That's all I'll admit to, Kate."

"The other day I was at Spikebuck treating a man badly burned in a fire at that freight yard," she said quite calmly.

"This man accused you of setting the fire. He said he saw you do it."

"Kate!" he breathed accusingly.

"So you didn't?"

He shook his head. "Why would I?" He paused, as though trying to think, then drawled wonderingly, "So that's why they burned me out!"

"I don't understand, Tom."

"That night my camp up there was fired. One of my men spotted your Captain Rold. Which is why I went to the trouble of getting him out of my way. Would you just sit back and take a thing like that, Kate?"

She didn't answer, trying to fit this bit of information into the puzzle of the rest. She was surprised that Bourke had made no mention of this. And now, deciding that Bourke had had a reason for not telling her about it, she looked around at Kimbrell, saying, "He accused you of other things, too."

"Let's have 'em."

"He said it was your man who shot up that stage last night, killing Red Drury and Hansen." She caught his surprised look. Then he was softly laughing as she went on, wanting to get it over with, "Later, he said, you killed this man to keep him from telling about it. And he's sure you killed his brother."

Kimbrell's laughter broke off. "Whose brother?"

"Bourke's."

"Your captain is the only man I've ever known by the name of Rold."

"Tom, please stop calling him my captain! His brother's name wasn't Rold. It was Frank Ames."

"And I'm supposed to have killed Ames?"

"According to him. It seems he got his information from one of your men today. Ben Spohr."

"So that's how Spohr got away!" he mused, giving her a wry glance. "Anything else?"

"No, that was all." Her voice was barely above a whisper.

Kimbrell gave her a wondering look. He jerked the reins, hauling the team down to a stand. "Kate!" he said in a low, bitter voice. "You actually believe it!"

125

He was staring at her with a look so guileless and stricken that she wanted to cry out that she hadn't for a moment believed any part of it. But just now a strange unaccountable stubbornness was in her, an emotion that had something to do with her feelings for Bourke. She wanted to speak, yet couldn't.

He drawled, "So I'm a killer."

"I didn't say that, Tom! I was merely repeating what Bourke told me. You deny it all?"

It was a long moment before he asked, quite gently, "Would you believe me if I did deny it?"

"Yes."

She wondered if she was telling the truth; for, though she hadn't willed it, there was a growing conviction in her that Bourke's story, strange as it was, had some basis in fact. Just how Bourke could be right and Tom Kimbrell innocent of the things he stood accused of she didn't know. But she had a wild hope now that this was the answer.

"Then I do deny it, Kate," he said quietly. "I did none of those things. Furthermore, I'm going to prove I didn't."

"Oh!" she breathed. "If you only could!"

He sawed at the team, turning them and then slapping them impatiently with the reins, heading back into town. And Kate was suddenly afraid, thinking of the possibility of his meeting Bourke. "Where are you going, Tom?"

"Out there to that wrecked stage to get Shaffer."

"But he's in town. I've just seen him."

He looked around at her with an expression she didn't understand, an oddly wary one. "How long ago?"

"Half an hour. He was at the house."

"Then I must have talked with him right afterward. It was just before I came to get you. He was on his way to the hills then."

He was turning the team into the cross-street leading to the river bridge now as she asked, "What help can Ben Shaffer be, Tom?"

"None, for sure. But if I can get him back here and find Rold we'll settle this."

Kate made no further protest, her relief keen at this postponement of any encounter between Bourke and Kimbrell. The buggy rattled across the planking of the bridge and beyond Kimbrell gave the team the whip and the animals settled into their swift mile-eating pace. It wasn't long before the road was beginning to twist in a gradual climb into the first of the Greenhorn foothills.

Presently Kimbrell said, "Better use the blanket, Kate. It's getting colder." Only then did she realize that she was almost shivering. She spread the blanket across her knees.

It was along the first stiff grade, with the blacks at a walk, that he casually asked, "Just what did Rold say helped him with his guesses?"

She tried to think back. "It was mostly what Ben Spohr told him."

He had no immediate comment to make on that; but presently he drawled, "Kate, I was holding Spohr for the sheriff when he got away. If you don't believe that, ask Shaffer when you see him."

"I'm not disbelieving you."

"I'd spoken to Red Drury about Spohr last night. And this morning I talked it over with Shaffer. Spohr was wanted for murder. Would you take the word of a man like that?"

"No," she admitted.

"Then why believe Rold when he repeats what Spohr told him?"

"Let's not talk about it," she said wearily. "I . . . I just don't know what to think."

"Spohr was a trouble maker. You know," . . . He was closely regarding her now . . . "the more I think of it, the more I believe he could have been saddling me with what he did himself. Take what happened to Frank Ames, for one. I've always thought there was something peculiar about that."

"How, Tom?"

"He'd been driving a wagon down to Spikebuck. When it got so late that they began wondering why he hadn't shown up, Ives sent a man out to look for him. This man found the wagon off the road and the horses grazing. The next day they found Ames in the river. I know about it because they had me in on the inquest."

She merely nodded and he went on, "Spohr was at my

127

camp in the canyon that night. He could have run onto Ames. What he had against him we'll never know. But we do know that Ames wasn't using his right name. Spohr could have known him before he came here, had some trouble with him."

"Yes, that could be," she agreed.

"Well, Spohr's long gone by now," he drawled. "So all we do is guess."

They had reached the crest of the rise and Kimbrell urged the team to a faster trot; and for the next twenty minutes neither of their voices spoke against the steady hoof-drum of the hurrying blacks.

Only when Kimbrell reined abruptly from the well-worn ruts of the main road and took a barely visible set of wheel-tracks branching to the right did Kate break the silence by quickly asking, "Where are we going?"

"Short-cut," he told her tersely. "There are a couple of places where we cross a creek. But it'll save us time." And now he stopped the team and lit the lamps.

There was a friendly glow alongside as they started on and Kate leaned back against the cushions again, her momentary apprehension gone. She was wondering what the night would bring, wondering too how long it would take them to find Bourke once they were back in Canon with the sheriff. She felt better about things now. Tom was proving out her faith in him and what he'd said about Spohr took some of the sting from Bourke's unbelievable accusations. Spohr had deceived Bourke, of course, and now there was a warmth, an excited expectancy in Kate over the prospect of being able to go to Bourke and smooth over their differences.

She recalled that moment when she had so hysterically told him of her thoughts of him, and felt her face go hot with shame. But then, with a stubborn pride, she knew she would never regret having said those things. They were true. She remembered vaguely having used the word love and now, consciously for the first time, she was wondering if she really could have become that interested in him.

Her thoughts stayed with Bourke for many minutes, finally to be jarred back to the moment by a particularly vicious jolt of the buggy. She was startled to see that they were headed down an incline so steep that the horses were barely able to keep the buggy from over-running them. Jackpine crowded closely on either side and big rocks littered the slope. There was no longer any sign of a road. Close ahead she caught the firefly flicker of the lamps reflected from water and as the team splashed into a stream seconds later she asked, "Are you sure this is the right way, Tom?"

"It smooths out up above," he told her, easing her worry.

He had to use the whip to get the horses up the far slope. Shortly they crossed a rolling meadow, heading for a dark margin of trees a good half-mile beyond. When they reached the timber they turned abreast it and after some minutes of smooth, fast going angled deep into a fold of the hills. They had come several miles since leaving the main road, Kate supposed, uneasily wishing she had a better idea of where they were.

Some minutes later Kimbrell climbed the buggy out along a ridge and followed it deeper into the hills. They crossed and recrossed another stream. It was a mile or so further on that Kimbrell drew rein.

"You're lost, Tom?" Kate's voice was anxious.

The lamplight strong on his face, she saw him smile broadly with a queer satisfied look. "Are you, Kate?"

She laughed uneasily. "I couldn't begin to tell you where we are."

"Good," he drawled.

She was trying to make sense of his unexpected word as he stepped aground. He began unhitching the team.

"What did you say, Tom?" she asked hesitantly.

"I said 'good.'"

She took that in with a strange disquiet striking through her. "That's a queer remark." She watched him working on the horses for several moments, finally asking, "What are you doing?"

"Leaving you."

Even before he added, "To walk home," a strong premonition of danger was striking through her. Then suddenly her mind brought something into sharp focus. The day-long confusion of her thoughts melted before a swift and terrible certainty; and she was afraid.

At once, in its entirety, she saw this act of Tom Kimbrell's for what it was. The next instant she was gasping, "So Bourke was right!"

He was unbuckling a breeching-strap on the off animal and waited until he had dropped it to turn and speak to her, drawling simply, "Every inch of the way."

"You meant to have Bourke killed last night," she said in a hushed voice. "Then afterward you shot the killer you'd hired!"

She caught his low laugh, heard him say, "Don't worry, Kate. No one will miss Bates."

"And Frank Ames?"

"The man was in my way," Kimbrell said, staring at her intently as he went on in a low grating voice, "The only thing that stood between me and a fortune. Imagine, Kate! Owning that freight outfit I could have called the turn, made 'em dance to my tune. There'd have been no limit to what they'd have paid me. They're throwing money to the winds up that canyon. What was wrong with my wanting a big chunk of it?"

When she remained silent, watching him wide-eyed and still afraid, he shrugged and turned his back on her. "That night Ames laughed at me, at my offer. Told me in so many words to go to hell. Men don't talk to me that way. We fought and ..." He shrugged. "If your captain hadn't come along I could still have won Cass Ives over. Then none of this would have happened. So," he added, "Rold's really to blame for most of it."

Kate waited a moment. When she was sure he wasn't going to say anything more, she murmured, "Dad had guessed part of it."

Kimbrell nodded. "Almost too much. If they'd listened to him at the inquest I might have had to pull out sooner. I was watching him, Kate, thinking he might have written Ames' family. Sure enough, he had."

The calmness of his admission made her tremble. The sure, swift moves of his hands took her glance and held it as they stripped the harness from both horses. She noticed he was leaving their bridles on and, as though he read her thought then, he drawled, "Better curl up and go to sleep right here. You have the blanket. You can make the road in half the time in the morning."

Now the fear that had been in her drained away to leave her all at once no longer afraid of him. Nor could she seem to summon more than a surface anger against him; for her fury, her rage, was deep inside her and lay strangely quiet, blanketed by her feeling of utter helplessness at how completely he had deceived her in bringing her to this isolated spot.

She wanted to kill Tom Kimbrell, she thought dispassionately. She would have gloried at finding a gun within her reach now as she said quietly, "Of course the sheriff's back in town. You simply lied when you said he'd ridden out here."

The lamplight let her catch his nod.

"The moment you're gone I'll start walking," she said.

"I expected that." He chuckled with a genuine amusement. "But all I need is two hours, Kate. Two hours and I'll be gone. After that they can spend a lot of time lookin' over a lot of country for me."

He was ready now, ready to leave, as he dropped the last length of harness and pulled himself up onto the back of one of the blacks. He reined the animal over alongside the buggy, leading the other through the tangle of harness lying in the grass.

He inclined his body forward in a bow that made a mockery of what he said: "So long, Kate. Can't help but wish this could have turned out differently for us, you and me."

The lamplight let him see the loathing and hate that blazed in her eyes. A broad smile made his face quite handsome as he drawled, "You've got a fire in you I like. Some man's going to be damned lucky. Rold, I wonder?"

When she made no reply he reined his horse on out and started away. She watched until the darkness had swallowed his shape. And after that she sat unmoving, listening until the hoof-echoes of his horses had died out along the ridge.

Only when the stillness was complete, when not a sound came to her, did a real anger begin to stir in Kate.

It mounted to a pitch that finally made her jump from the buggy and start running in the direction Kimbrell had taken, calling his name. It was the sound of her voice finally that sobered her to the realization of how futile her action was. She stopped and stood staring off into the blackness, breathing heavily, thinking now of the things she should have told him, of how contemptible and cowardly and loathsome he was.

She turned finally and walked back toward the buggy, its lamps guiding her. And now for the first time she was realizing how completely helpless Kimbrell had left her. She knew she must be miles from the Greenhorn road; she had been too deep in her thoughts to notice directions and she hadn't the beginning of an idea on which way she should walk to get back to the road. She was completely and utterly lost.

But, regardless of that, it didn't once occur to her to spend the night here as Kimbrell had suggested. Remembering what time it had been when they left town, guessing on how long the drive here had taken them, she supposed it must now be a little past seven. Perhaps, she decided, if she walked east and managed to reach the road it wouldn't be too late to rule out the chance of meeting someone travelling along it. It might take her an hour or two, possibly three. And even if she met no one and had to walk all the way back to town it would be better than spending the night here.

The possibility that the road might be a great deal nearer than she realized was what made her hurry to the buggy now and lift one of the lamps from its socket. Holding it by its post, she took a long look at the stars to judge her direction, then left the buggy.

It was grassy here along the ridge and she had gone less than a hundred yards before she began to feel the dampness of dew about her ankles. Her skirt was in the way and she stopped long enough to gather its hem and her petticoat and tuck them into her belt. After that the walking was easier.

After going on some three minutes she came to a small clump of pine and brush, noticing a tall dead giant greybark rising over the other trees, its tangle of bare branches climbing into the obscurity above the reach of her lamp. And she had gone well past it, far out across the grassy crest of the ridge, before the thought struck her.

That thought sent her hurrying back, retracing her steps to that small island of timber. Coming up on it again she walked around it, finding that it was well isolated from any other trees. The lamp-glow showed her nothing but a long reach of ankle-high grass stretching away on all sides. Time and again her glance would go to that stately dead pine rising over the others.

When she finally walked into the thickets and started gathering dead branches she was wondering if her idea wasn't after all a waste of time. But she couldn't help remembering the men who must be up there somewhere along the Greenhorn road at the wrecked stage.

She worked steadily for twenty minutes, setting the lamp at the base of the grey-bark's three-foot-thick trunk. Close by were several dead saplings. She broke them off and dragged them in to the big tree and piled them against its trunk. Presently she had a mound of dead brush almost as high as her waist. Underneath the nearby pines she found a matting of dry needles and gathered handfuls of them in her skirt, throwing them on the pile of brush. Far back, almost beyond the lantern's reach, she discovered a rotting windfall and pulled loose a length of its pitchy upper side and dragged it to throw on top of the smaller branches.

Then came the minute that counted most. She unscrewed the lamp's base and emptied all the coal-oil from it onto the thickest bed of needles. Taking off a shoe, she smashed all the glass in the lamp, being careful not to put out the wick's flame. Finally she laid the lamp's frame on the oil-soaked needles, pushing some of them up into the frame and against the blazing wick.

The coal-oil caught suddenly, furiously, scorching her hand before she could draw it away. Then, gradually those first leaping flames died back. She started fanning the fire with her skirt. It built up again slowly but surely until some of the larger branches started burning.

When the pitch log finally caught and began blazing, Kate turned away and walked out through the trees and into the grass. She sat down, at first seeing only a feeble glow shining through the scrub-oak thickets. That glow grew brighter. Suddenly flames were leaping above the height of the thickets, reaching for the dead lower branches of the big pine.

A forest fire was a dread thing in these timber-blanketed hills. From a distance this one would seem to be threatening acres of trees.

Now there was nothing for Kate to do but wait—and hope that someone would see the blaze.

Seven

SOME CLAIMED LATER that De Remer planned what happened that night; others, De Remer's friends, insisted it was just a natural blowing off of steam against the Sante Fe's high-handedness—their having brought in Masterson and his toughs to cow the opposition, their taking advantage of the lease on the Rio Grande to let its rolling stock go to pieces, their favoring Eastern shippers by the prohibitive rates set on freight coming south from Denver. Whatever the reason, an hour after dark that night boulders began dropping off of the rim into the Gorge directly on the Sante Fe camp at Twelve Mile Bridge.

Men who had fought at Gettysburg claimed later that it was worse than the first day's cannonading there. These boulders dropped five hundred, a thousand feet straight down to shatter thunderingly against ledges or carom off the bare granite slopes, their fragments plummeting like grapeshot to the bottom of the abyss, each report of rock on rock waking a dozen mighty echoes striking back and forth across the depths. It was a nightmare out of hell for the men below. They saw two meteor-like chunks of the red granite raise twenty-foot geysers of spray from the roaring Arkansas within a wagon's length of the bridge. Twelve Mile's girders streamed water, it shook against its foundations. But after it was over, when the river's perpetually raging voice heightened the merciful stillness, the bridge was standing.

Two mules were killed, a cook's pots and pans were dented and twisted as though made of paper, one tent had collapsed and shrouded a boulder half as big as a locomotive and the freshly mounded grade was cratered like a Moonscape over a four hundred yard stretch of its length. Not a man was hurt.

But more than one man's temper was at the boil. Without orders, grabbing any weapon at hand—guns, clubs, even broken bottles—some thirty-odd guards and grade workers piled onto a flatcar, hooked a locomotive to it and started down the Gorge. At the camp near its mouth they picked up another dozen hot-heads. Later, they dropped off the flatcar at the upper end of town and in a body cruised down Main looking for trouble. But, strangely, the town was quiet and the street nearly deserted. They roughed up two townsmen and, discovering their mistake barely in time, sobered somewhat. The Rio Grande had evidently been expecting some such play and was lying low. So the Sante Fe men retired to the saloons to pickle their grudge in alcohol and save it for another day.

At about the time the street went quiet again a fast-running horse crossing Main along Sixth laid a swift-cadenced echo down the thoroughfare. Tom Kimbrell turned his black in at the livery corral not even bothering to remove the animal's bridle before he closed the gate and made off down the walk. After he had gone the horse just stood there, head down and glistening flanks heaving, too tired to move across to the watering trough. The black would never again be worth the price of the feed to keep him.

Going along Main, Kimbrell kept glancing furtively behind him. He slowed each time he saw someone ahead of him and, at Fourth, turned down past Alling's Hardware and into the alley behind it. Halfway through to the next block he pushed open a door and stepped into a saloon's dimly lit store-room. Curtains closing off the end of the bar let through so much light that he didn't dare part them in the middle but stepped to one side, in behind the partition, before inching open the material to peer into the smoke-fogged room beyond. It was quiet in there—the Sante Fe men had gone further down-street—with a low hum of voices, the clink of glasses, the occasional thump of one of the beer-taps working.

Kimbrell's survey of the room lasted three minutes; afterward he left the place as unobtrusively as he had entered.

The four men Shaffer had left to search the canyon below the wrecked stage were finishing supper along the road above when Al Rush, along with the man the sheriff had sent to Silver Cliff after him, came riding down on the fire.

The old scout was hungry after his long ride and somewhat disdainful of the need for any hurry in setting about his chore. So the others had to watch him eat and then get a cigar going before he finally rose and stretched to ask tartly, "Now how much do you know for sure about this?"

"Next to nothin'," one of them answered. He stepped over to the edge of the road with a lantern, holding it out so that the wreck showed 'way below, almost out of sight. "Just take a look. How could a man ride that thing down there and walk away from it?"

"No sign at all?" Rush queried, not liking the inference that he had come all these miles for nothing.

"Sure there's sign. Just below. Some ranny waited down there in the trees for the stage and rode out alongside it. We—"

"I know all that," Rush cut in. "But what've you run across since noon?"

"Nothin'," one of the others said.

So Rush, with an irritable shrug, started picking his way carefully down the slope. He was never at his ease afoot and not so nimble as he once had been; and time and again they stopped to wait for him. But finally he reached the wreck and started looking around.

He wanted to know just how Red Drury's body had been lying, just where they had found the driver; he asked a lot of other questions that seemed quite pointless. Still, they showed him a lot of respect, for one of them who was old enough to remember had told the rest what a fine figure of a man Rush had made forty years ago with his fringed buckskins, the quillwork moccasins and his long hair braided Indian-fashion. So, tired as they were, anxious as they were to finish this and get back to Canon, they didn't try to hurry him.

The last thing he did at the Concord was to lift the poncho off the broken spoke of a wheel where it had hung since late morning, asking, "What's this?"

"It was layin' up there above. Must've been thrown out when she went over."

Rush muttered, "Hm-m," and squatted down to turn the poncho inside out. The stain on the inside of the right sleeve was plain enough, unmistakably that of dried blood. Yet none of them had thought to look for it and when he asked, "Was this man hurt before he took the tumble?" they shook their heads and looked at one another accusingly, as though asking why someone hadn't had the brains to do what the old man was doing.

It was much the same up on the ledge and then above under the pines twenty minutes later when they took him up there to show him the prints of the killer's horse. Rush kept cursing the lantern's poor light; but before they knew it he was reading a different story than they had.

He told it to them as he hunkered down in the middle of the road, pointing to a certain track he had picked from the many showing there. "This critter was the one he rode away."

"Who?"

"The man you're looking for. Drury's prisoner."

They didn't make much sense of it, although the inferences to what he was saying jolted them. One man protested feebly. "Hell, we been down in that gulch lookin' for his body all afternoon."

"Can't help it," Rush drawled. "He was hurt, his right arm bleedin'. The off-lead animal came out of the smash-up standin'. Your man led the horse up here, had his look at what we been lookin' at, then rode on back down. Toward the end of the storm, I'd reckon." Then he added caustically, "Though God knows how I can be sure, the way you've messed up the sign millin' around here all day. That all you wanted to know?"

One of them whistled softly, breathing, "You said it!"

But another put in quickly, "One thing more. This first man now, the one that stopped the stage. Could he have been a side-kick of Rold's?"

"Seems I forgot to bring along my crystal ball," was Rush's dry rejoinder. "Anything else?"

"No. This'll do us. And much obliged. In case you're interested, Rush, you've just put a rope around a man's neck."

"That's his lookout," Al Rush drawled.

Presently he went on up the road alone, back toward Silver Cliff. And Shaffer's men didn't waste much time starting for Canon, although the old scout's deliberateness seemed to have infected them. They weren't hurrying. There was plenty of time for what they had to do.

They had covered two twisting downward miles when the man in the lead spotted a cherry-red glow shining against the black backdrop of the lower foothills directly to the north. They all pulled in, watching the fire silently for a brief interval, seeing it build higher until suddenly the orange torch of a pine being gutted by the flames leaped into plain sight.

"There's a night's work cut out for us," one of them drawled finally.

"Hell, let 'er burn!" growled the man alongside.

"And maybe see the whole slope go? Don't be a damn' fool!"

"We could split up," suggested another. "Two go over there, two to town."

"One man's enough to send in. Brother, that blaze is goin' to take some stoppin'. Now why'd we have to run onto this along with what we've already got?"

None of them liked the prospect of having to fight a forest fire and they sat watching it for another minute or so, trying to think of a way around their obvious duty. But there was no way out of it and finally the lead man said," Okay, see you in a couple hours."

He went on down the road at a stiff trot and when he

was out of sight the other three cut down through the pines, riding point for the fire.

Tom Kimbrell entered the second saloon as he had the first, by its alley door. This time he was uncomfortably exposed in a well-lighted poker alcove. He nodded to a couple of acquaintances but didn't approach the tables. A woman in a purple dress with an ostrich feather clipped to one shoulder-strap came on back and spoke to him.

He ignored what she said, asking, "Seen Murray Simmons around tonight, Mary?"

"He was here earlier. Try Milt's place, honey. Say, when are we going to have an ev ning?"

"Any day now," was his rejoinder. And he turned to the door.

Kimbrell found Simmons in the fourth saloon he visited. Although he spotted his quarry almost at once he carefully eyed the room before going up to him at the bar.

Even there he was wary, his glance roving restlessly as he came close in behind Simmons and quietly spoke to him. "Want to see you, Murray. Back here."

He was already turning away when Simmons' answer came. "Like hell!"

Kimbrell stopped, looked around at the man. "You won't regret it, Murray."

He didn't wait for a further word but stepped on back along the bar and into the short hallway between two private gaming rooms. He could see Simmons still standing where he had left him and it irritated him that the man found it necessary to go through this preliminary before joining him. They had exchanged some heated words about six hours ago, shortly after Kimbrell had the word of Bourke's visit to the tie camp and of Spohr's escape. Now Kimbrell was gambling on Simmons having enough curiosity over the matter they had been discussing to want to discuss it further.

His gamble paid off several minutes later when Simmons deliberately turned and looked his way, then picked up his half-empty glass and came on back.

When the man stood in front of him, Kimbrell drawled, "I can shade the price a bit tonight, Murray."

"It'll take more than a bit," came the other's uncompromising rejoinder. His hand lifted and he ran a forefinger along his wide moustaches.

"You offered five, I asked ten. Now if—"

"Five for the mills and the contract," Simmons reminded him dryly.

"No deal," Kimbrell said. "I might take ten for the mills alone. Might even throw in the camp there on the river. But now—"

"The hell with your camp! I hear it's mostly burned out anyway." Simmons smiled crookedly. "What happened? One of your boys just keepin' in practice? How do you like being on the hot end of a blaze? Like the one you lit for me before you crowded me out!"

"Watch it, Murray!" Kimbrell drawled, stung by this allusion to something that had considerable foundation in fact. "I could take exception to that."

"Take it! Who cares?"

Kimbrell made a definite effort to bridle his temper now. "I said I'd throw in the river yard. How about it?"

"And the contract. And for five, not ten."

"Look, Murray. You—" Kimbrell had said this much before realizing the utter futility of arguing. He knew Murray Simmons to be a stubborn man. And time was running out on him.

So he said, "Okay, it's yours for five."

Simmons was so surprised he took half a step backward. "You in your right mind, Tom?"

"Told you I was leaving."

"Sure. But—" Simmons' jaw clamped shut as he realized he was arguing against himself. "Then it's settled?"

Kimbrell nodded. "If you can get the money tonight."

"Tonight! God A'mighty, man, I don't carry a wad like that with me! Why all the hurry?"

"Because a chance like this doesn't come often," Kimbrell told him. "Because I want to be in Leadville by noon tomorrow. Why do you suppose I sneaked in here this way?"

"Didn't want to be seen, I reckon."

"I didn't. You're the only man who knows about this, Murray. If anyone else gets wind of it I'll be followed and ten to one someone beats me taking out a lease on that claim."

Simmons shook his head uncomprehendingly. "Maybe you know what you're doin'. I don't. What makes you think you know anything about a silver mine?"

"You leave that to me. I didn't know much about tie-cutting when I showed up here, did I?"

"Enough," Simmons drawled with unmistakable meaning.

"Aren't you satisfied? Don't you know you'll clear twenty thousand on this contract alone? Don't—"

"Sure, sure," the other said hastily.

"Then get the money. Now."

"Where?"

"Borrow it. Try Milt. Or Jordan. Your word's good with either of them."

Simmons frowned, trying to think. Here was an opportunity that came to a man once in a lifetime. He had taken a licking from Kimbrell less than a year ago, had been forced to sell his tie-mill. Now he had the chance of buying his old one back along with four others, a leased yard on the river, a contract for thirty thousand crossties —all for a song.

He turned and looked toward the front of the room, saying disappointedly, desperately almost, "Jordan's just gone."

"You know where he lives. Or try Milt. He keeps twice that much in his safe."

Simmons pulled his coat together and buttoned it. A real excitement was beginning to show in him. "Where'll I meet you?"

"My hotel room in half an hour. I'll have deeds, bills of sale, everything."

"And the contract," Simmons drawled as he turned away.

Almost the first man Cass saw as he shouldered in through the bat-wing doors of the St. Julian was Jim Manlove. He went up to the blacksmith asking, "Any luck?"

"Not a bit." Manlove's look was a worried one. His fingers kept turning a half-emptied shotglass of whiskey sitting on the bar before him.

Cass caught the apron's eye, nodded, and reached out to stop a bottle and glass that shortly came sliding down to him. He filled the glass, emptied it at a gulp and refilled it.

Jim Manlove watched all this with a growing wonder. for Cass wasn't a drinking man. And finally the blacksmith said, "I'd go easy on that stuff. It'll make your hair fall out."

Cass ignored the remark. He was frowning now as he said, "Jim, try and think back. Just what did Rold do there at the yard this afternoon?"

"Asked for you first."

"Then what?"

"Talked with Dan a minute or so. Told him he'd better lay off a few more days. Then he went into the office and wrote these two letters I gave you."

Cass nodded. "One for me, the other for De Remer. Did he say how he happened to know De Remer?"

"No."

"And he didn't mention this trouble he's in?"

"Not a word of it."

Cass shook his head, drank half the whiskey in his glass. "His arm was hurt?"

"It sure looked like it."

Cass drew in a long breath, let it out slowly, audibly. "It beats me. Half the town would like to believe he did those killings and got away."

"And the other half already does believe it."

"Jim, I'm worried. Worried as I've ever been," Cass drawled solemnly. "What can we do for him?"

"Find him, first of all."

"You looked where I asked you to?"

"Those places and more."

Abruptly Cass's frown eased. He said, "The Banks girl!"

"What about her?"

"She might know where he is." Cass was turning from the bar, heading for the doors as he spoke.

As he hurried on through the block and turned up

River Street toward the Banks house, he was wondering if he shouldn't have confided in Jim Manlove. But Bourke's brief note, telling of the killings and of Tom Kimbrell being behind them, had asked him not to tell anyone what he knew. Bourke probably hadn't known then how badly things were going to turn for him. The town was talking of nothing but the murders tonight; and some of it was lynch talk. It was almost too much to ask of Jim Manlove that he take his, Cass's, word for it that Bourke was blameless in all this without explaining.

Now, as he came within sight of the Banks house and saw lamplight shining from one of the rear windows, Cass was somewhat encouraged. But after he had knocked at the front door without getting an answer his worries crowded in on him again. Presently he went down the side path and rapped there. Still no sound came from the house. Finally he tried the door, found it unlocked and opened it long enough to call, "Anyone home?"

Nothing but the slow ticking of the clock against the stillness answered him.

Wearily now, he turned back up the street and across to Main, deciding to spend the night at the hotel. He was abreast a store's darkened front when a voice spoke his name out of the door's setback.

It was Bourke.

"I'll be damned!" was all Cass could think of to say as he hauled up short.

"So will I," came Bourke's drawl from the shadows. "Thought I told you to stay clear of this, Cass."

"That was this afternoon—before you knew how this was building up. Bourke, they'd string you up tonight if they could lay hands on you!"

"Is it that bad?"

A vast impatience struck through Cass. He was worried, tormented at the thought of the possibilities. Now his anger was rising as he asked, "Why loaf here right smack in the middle of 'em?"

"There's something to lean against, I can see both walks and it's too early to turn in."

That sobered Cass. He knew now why Bourke was waiting here and asked quietly, "Kimbrell?"

Bourke said nothing for a moment. Then came his slow drawl, "It's a nice night, Cass."

"I know," Cass said mildly. "And it'll more than likely be warmer tomorrow." He was barely able to make out Bourke's high shape there in the gloom. "Have you seen him?"

"Would I be here if I had?"

Cass sighed helplessly. "It's late, Bourke. You could use some sleep."

"Later," Bourke said tonelessly.

The full realization that he could do nothing about this came to Cass just then. Bourke was stubborn. He had seen that. But so was he stubborn and now he made a last try at changing Bourke's mind. "Look," he said. "This is playing it on long odds. A couple hundred men in this town would like to let daylight through you. And a—"

"And those couple hundred don't know me from Adam," Bourke cut in. "Save your wind, Cass."

"Get that arm so it'll work before you go after him!" Cass flared. "Then get the sheriff and take him with you. Right now you're in bad shape."

"You're a worrier."

Cass sighed. He had known how useless it was to argue. "All right," he said quietly, "what can I do to help?"

"Find Kimbrell."

"Where?"

"If I knew I'd be there, Cass."

"What about his room?"

"Where is it?"

"The hotel. Top floor."

"Thanks." Bourke stepped out of the deeper shadow.

Panicked, Cass reached out and put a hand to Bourke's chest, pushing him deeper into the doorway. "Use your head, man! You can't just walk in there."

"I can try."

Cass shook his head violently. "You can't! I'll go have a look. I'll be right back. You wait."

He didn't give Bourke the chance to answer, stepping

out onto the walk once more. Half a dozen strides away he looked back. Bourke wasn't following and a keen relief struck through him as he went on.

He climbed the stairs to the *McClure House* lobby and went straight to the desk, asking the clerk, "Tom in?"

"Tom who?"

"Kimbrell."

"Try thirty-eight. Next floor up."

Cass looked the lobby over carefully as he crossed it, making a slight detour to inspect two couches that sat with their backs to him. Kimbrell wasn't in the lobby and Cass headed for the stairs to the top floor. He was approaching them when he noticed a man coming down toward him. After a single cursory glance, which told him that this man was neither so broad nor so tall as Kimbrell, Cass at once forgot him.

He started up the steps and the man on his way down, coming abreast him, stopped and said, "Not speakin' to your friends tonight, Cass?"

Cass really looked at the other for the first time now and, seeing who it was, said, "Hiyuh, Murray. How goes it?"

"Pretty damn good," Murray Simmons said. As Cass started on, he reached out and laid a hand on his arm, bursting out, "Lord, I've got to tell someone! It might as well be you, since we'll be doing business together."

"Not now, Murray," Cass said impatiently. "Got something on my mind."

"Well, here's something to put along with it," Murray said hurriedly. "Tom Kimbrell's sold me his layout. The whole shootin' match, plus his contract."

Cass's head came sharply around. "Say that again."

"Okay, call me a liar. But it's gospel. I've bought Kimbrell out. Just a minute ago. For a song."

Cass looked quickly up the stairway. "He's up in his room?"

"Just left him."

At Murray's answer, Cass turned and went back down the steps. Murray called, "Hold on!" but Cass kept on going.

He hurried out of the lobby and down to the street.

On the walk out front he abruptly halted, struck by the thought that what he was about to do might be costing a man his life. If it was Bourke's life, he would never forgive himself. But then his reasoning took an odd turn. Bourke was trusting him, and to betray that trust by denying that Kimbrell was at the hotel might be the worst thing he could do for Bourke. He had a queer presentiment that Bourke and Kimbrell were to meet regardless of anything he could do and, believing that, he knew now that it lay within his power to give Bourke the advantage.

So he went on down the walk as far as the doorway where Bourke waited, stopping there to say soberly, "He's there. Up in his room."

Bourke at once came toward him out of the shadows, asking, "Which one?"

"Thirty-eight. Top floor," Cass said. "I'll go with you."

Bourke shook his head. "Not this time, Cass. But thanks. Thanks a lot."

"That's what I thought you'd say." Cass sighed. "Well, don't waste any time. And don't give him a chance. He must be clearing out. He's sold everything to a man I know, Murray Simmons."

Bourke gave him a quizzical glance. "Everything?"

"So Murray said. Even to his contract."

"Then you'd better tear open that letter I left for De Remer. Had I told you I was working for him?"

"No."

Bourke nodded. "He was paying me to keep an eye on Kimbrell. You can add a line to what I wrote him. Tell him they'll be dealing with this Simmons from now on, that Kimbrell's sold out. And ask him to let the general know I sent this word."

"You can damn' well do it yourself," Cass said with a pointed meaning.

Bourke smiled. "Come to think of it, I can," he drawled. Then he stepped on past Cass and up the walk.

It struck Bourke as something of an omen—bad or good, he couldn't decide which—that he should be concluding this unwanted piece of business for De Remer, for Palmer, at the last possible moment. This afternoon there at Canyon Line's office he'd written De Remer the letter, telling him as much as Ben Spohr had known of Kimbrell's dealings with the Sante Fe so far. He had mentioned nothing beyond that, nothing of the possibility of Kimbrell leaving. Now either Cass or he would take care of that, adding whatever was necessary to inform De Remer of the outcome of the affair.

He didn't turn in at the *McClure House's* lighted stairway entrance but kept on to the corner, taking the side street as he had earlier tonight. He had that strong reminder of his visit to Eleanor as he turned into the kitchen entrance. The kitchen was practically dark now, lit by only one turned-down gas jet over the dish tubs beyond the sink. The stale trapped air in here wasn't good and he climbed quickly out of it, pausing as he reached the second floor landing.

A low murmur of voices drifted to him from out in the lobby. He though idly of walking to the corridor's bend and looking into the big room on the chance of seeing Eleanor; yet the thought died almost at once without stirring even a remote emotion in him beyond faint curiosity. He doubted that she had taken the train. It would be typical of her to wait on here hoping for the chance to see him; for by now she must be regretting what she had said and done, trying to see a way of making amends and at the same time come out of this blameless. The thought struck him that Kate Banks would never have tried a deception like Eleanor's. And now a real regret was in him at remembering how confused and baffling had been that talk with Kate this evening. He wanted very much to see her again, to try once more to explain.

He turned to that second flight of steps and, halfway up them, drew his hand from his shirt. He could feel the swelling and the stiffness as he straightened the bad arm. He flexed his fingers. The joints ached. But there was strength enough in them to give him a firm grip when he lifted the Colt's clear of his belt.

He went on with the gun in hand, the worn treads squeaking under his weight so that he gave up trying to walk soundlessly and climbed deliberately to the upper stair-head.

At the precise moment he stepped into that feebly lit

upper corridor, a light slanting from an inched-open door close ahead suddenly blacked out.

He had nothing but that—the turning out of that light —to account for an instant's wariness settling through him. He stood there briefly telling himself that his nerves were on edge, that the narrow wedge of darkness staring at him from the slit of the door meant nothing. Kimbrell's room was somewhere on this floor. This probably wasn't even his door. He tried to make out the numbering on the panel, couldn't; yet the wariness built more strongly in him.

The Colt's hung at his side away from the door and as he stepped on down the hall he was careful to keep that arm from swinging. He came even with the door. And now he could faintly see the brass numbers on its upper panel. He made out a 3, then the 8.

38!

Suddenly it came to him that Kimbrell was in there and in that instant he swung to face the door. He lifted a boot and kicked it open.

Its sharp backswing jarred hard into something. There came a startled low cry out of which Bourke somehow recognized the tone of Kimbrell's voice. Then he lunged into the room.

Powder-flame scorched the back of his neck and a thunderclap explosion deafened him. On the heel of that sound he threw his body sideways with his bad arm lifting toward the blackness out of which the shot had come. A numbing blow beat his arm down and the Colt's went spinning from his hand. Instinctively he brought his left arm arcing around in a savage swing. His fist connected solidly with something that yielded slightly. Then Kimbrell's shape staggered into the door's feebly lit rectangle.

Bourke wheeled, trying to knee the man in the groin. Kimbrell sensed what was coming and doubled over, taking the force of the blow in the abdomen. His hands came open as the pain hit him and his gun struck the floor and he stumbled into it, kicking it into the blackness across the room. He came staggering against Bourke before Bourke could lift his arms. He was dazed by that first blow, now gagging for breath from that vicious knee-lift. He had his head low against Bourke's chest and his arms closed around Bourke's waist in a fierce grip that drove Bourke's wind out of him.

Bourke spread his boots and suddenly swung his upper body around. The force of the swing carried Kimbrell off balance. His hold didn't break. They both fell out through the door.

Kimbrell had the advantage in the fall. He was on top, he ducked his head and when they hit the floor the top of his skull drove upward against Bourke's chin. Momentarily, Bourke's long frame went limp. Kimbrell, pressing his advantage, let go his hold and tried to sit astride his victim.

Bourke somehow summoned the strength to lift a boot and shove out from the wall. Kimbrell tried to fall on him again but he twisted from under the man and got to his feet. Before he was quite erect Kimbrell made a dive for his legs.

He went over backward, Kimbrell on hands and knees coming after him. He rolled sharply to the side, realized too late that he was lying at the head of the stairway. Then he was falling.

He tried to double up as he rolled down the stairs. The edge of one step caught him between the shoulders and a knifelike pain stabbed the length of his spine. He heard the racket of his boots hitting the wall, of his shoulders springing the treads as faraway sounds. He piled up at the bottom of the steps and hit the wall with his back and the plaster gave way and came showering about him.

Then Kimbrell came pounding down toward him, taking the steps two, sometimes three, at a time. Bourke got his feet under him and came to a crouch and when Kimbrell's boot was reaching down to the fourth step above he dove for the man's legs.

Kimbrell tried to kick him in the face; instead his boot slammed into Bourke's bad shoulder, sending a paralysis through him all the way to his hips. Kimbrell's momentum carried him on over in a diving fall and his head and shoulders drove into the wall below.

For a moment neither of them moved. Then Bourke rolled over slowly. He dazedly heard someone shout something along the hallway above. His vision brought Kimbrell into focus. And then he was pushing to his feet, seeing Kimbrell straightening his legs and looking up at him.

Kimbrell tried to crawl away. Bourke stepped in on him, stumbled and tried to fall on the man knees-first. He missed and rolled out into the main hallway and was coming to his knees when Kimbrell hit him from behind with a driving blow that connected high at the back of his head. He reached out for the corridor's wall, bracing himself as he came erect. On his way up Kimbrell struck him once more, low in the back over the kidneys.

The pain seemed to be all through him now as he stumbled around. He saw Kimbrell's fist arcing toward his face and ducked his head and shoved out from the wall. All the weight of his shoulders behind them, he drove two blows in at Kimbrell's waist. Fire streaked up his bad right arm and now the man crowded into him and he managed to rake one of his shins with a boot.

That sent Kimbrell backward a step and in the two seconds they stood apart Bourke realized he was beaten if he continued to fight this way. Kimbrell's bull-like strength was too much for him with the handicap of his bad arm. Kimbrell would wear him down, then gouge him, cripple him, cut him to ribbons.

So now as Kimbrell crouched and came at him, Bourke caught his balance and sidestepped, jabbing the man lightly in the face with his left. Kimbrell wasted strength trying to brush that left aside and, seeing an opening, Bourke threw his right at Kimbrell's ear, ignoring the pain it cost him. The blow connected and Kimbrell drew away. They circled each other, Bourke surprised to glimpse fleetingly the lobby end of the hallway crowded with onlookers.

Kimbrell charged once more, coming in fast. Again Bourke sidestepped, drew the man off his balance, then let him have a long hard uppercut in the face. The blow stunned Kimbrell and he staggered on past and into the head of a short cross-corridor that ended at a window overlooking the sidestreet twenty feet away.

Kimbrell wheeled sharply around as Bourke followed. He threw a vicious choppy left swing that missed Bourke and carried his fist into the wall. His face was bleeding now at mouth and nose and he grimaced with the pain of his hurt hand. Yet as Bourke closed on him he whipped in a wicked right that beat aside Bourke's guard, the bad arm, and caught him at the pit of the stomach. Bourke forgot himself for a moment and they stood close, neither giving an inch, throwing wild blows that damaged neither beyond opening a gash across Bourke's left cheek.

Bourke caught himself looking down once as he ducked under one of Kimbrell's roundhouse swings. He saw the man's boot, he stepped on it, he straightened and fell shoulder-first into Kimbrell.

There was nothing Kimbrell could do to keep himself from falling. He tried to catch a hold on Bourke but Bourke swung away. Then, as Kimbrell went over backward, Bourke wheeled in on him and caught him twice in the face with hard stiff uppercuts.

Kimbrell was moaning softly as he got to his feet. There was a sunken-in look to his left cheek where Bourke's knuckles had broken the bone. He saw what was coming and tried to get his arms up. Bourke hit a fraction of a second too soon for him and his head snapped sideways into the wall. It was the wall that kept him from falling. He staggered two steps to catch himself, trying to wheel around. He was close to the window now. Bourke hit him again, knuckles smashing against his ear to set up a roaring in his head. He lowered his head and brought up his arms to protect himself, Bourke reached out, knocked his arms down, then lifted him erect with a long hard blow to the chin.

Kimbrell screamed hoarsely as his head rocked back. He wanted to get down on his knees, on his stomach, anything to get out of Bourke's way. But Bourke didn't let him. He hit him twice in the chest to push him backward another step.

That step put the sill of the window against the back

of Kimbrell's knees. He sensed what was coming and groped to either side with his hands.

Bourke took his time, cocking his shoulders, drawing his arm far back, pausing to try for a full breath. He had never swung so hard at anything—with club, axe or fist. He felt one of his knuckles go when his hand smashed into Kimbrell's face at the bridge of the nose.

Kimbrell's heavy frame went backward through the window. The glass shattered apart, jangled to the floor. The window's sill caught him at the knees. Two feet outward across the narrow balcony the low iron railing hit the small of his back. He teetered there a moment, head thrown back, arms flailing. Then as Bourke reached out trying to catch one of his boots, Kimbrell cartwheeled on out into the night and dropped from sight.

They half carried, half walked Bourke into the lobby and eased him into a chair. Someone brought a basin of water and began wiping his face. He sat with his eyes closed and at first was aware only of the delicious coolness of his face, of the smarting pain as someone swabbed at his cuts and bruises.

As from a great distance he heard a man saying, ". . . good thing it was his back broken now instead of our having to break his neck later." There was a confusion of other voices. Bourke didn't want to listen to them. He wanted to sleep, nothing else.

Then a voice close, very close to him, said gently, "Bourke."

His tiredness seemed to ease away a little. He opened his eyes. Kate was kneeling there in front of him. There was a brightness in her eyes, a tenderness more eloquent than words could ever have been. And suddenly he knew that he loved this girl.

"Better now?" she asked.

"Considerable."

"Everything's all right, Bourke. Do you understand?"

He managed a nod.

"Tom admitted everything to me, Bourke. He took me miles out into the country and left me. I started a fire and those men who'd been up there where you were last night saw it and . . ."

Her words trailed off as she saw what his eyes were trying to tell her. She breathed wonderingly, so softly he could hardly hear, "Why, Bourke! I didn't know."

He had no trouble at all lifting his arms now. And it seemed very right that she came into them.

This Bantam Book contains the complete text of the original edition. Not one word has been changed or omitted. The low-priced Bantam edition is made possible by the large sale and effective promotion of the original edition, published by Dodd, Mead & Company, Inc.

- *Desert and mountain*
  - *Grassy valley and rocky ridge*
    - *Cowtown and dance hall*
      - *Dry farm and one-loop spread*
- *Ramrod and rannihan*
  - *Gun-slinger and sheriff*
    - *Cavalry and Indians*
      - *Dude and old-timer*

THE DRAMA OF THE OLD WEST LIVES AGAIN IN

BANTAM WESTERNS

FRESH! **AUTHENTIC!** **LIVELY!**

Look for
**BANTAM
WESTERNS**
wherever
BANTAM BOOKS
are sold